5.00

By BOB GOOCH

P9-CDV-262

bass fishing

STRIPERS, WHITE BASS, YELLOW BASS AND PERCH

TIDEWATER PUBLISHERS   •   1975

Cambridge, Maryland

Library of Congress Cataloging in Publication Data

Gooch, Bob, 1919-
　　Bass fishing.

　　Includes index.
　　1. Striped bass fishing. 2. White bass fishing.
3. White perch fishing. 4. Yellow bass fishing.
I. Title.
SH691.S7G66　　　　799.1'7'58　　　　75—17965
ISBN 0—87033—206-6

ACKNOWLEDGMENTS

I am deeply grateful for the unselfish assistance of many people who helped me gather the wide variety of material necessary for a book of this nature. We share a common interest in the true basses and the vital and continuing roles these fish are destined to play in our environment and the future of angling in America. This interest was dramatically demonstrated by the willingness with which they responded to my requests for information accessible to them.

Dedicated professional fishery biologists of the state fish and game agencies throughout the United States completed my questionnaires, filling me in on the status of the true basses in each of the 50 states. They also volunteered much additional general and detailed information in the form of research papers and reports. The information they and various outdoor writers gave me on their respective states is condensed in Chapter 3, *The Bass States.* Even the negative replies from the states to which the true basses are not native—nor have not as yet been introduced—were also helpful in establishing the bass' natural and adopted ranges. From these responses I was also able to develop a trend as to the future prospects for the fish in heretofore untried waters.

Particularly valuable were research papers from the fishery departments of the states of Alabama, Arizona, Arkansas, California, Colorado, Florida, Illinois, Louisiana, Maine, Massachusetts, Nebraska, New Jersey, New York, North Carolina, Ohio, Oklahoma, Pennsylvania, Rhode Island, South Carolina, Tennessee, Texas and Virginia. Much of the information contained in Chapter 5 on the management of the true basses came from these excellent reports.

Fellow outdoor writers Mike Hershberger of Alaska, Tom Foust of Arizona, Harry Bonner of California, Bill Baab of Georgia, William Radke of Illinois, Hank Bradshaw of Iowa, Cal O'Brien of Maine, Don Carpenter of Maryland, Henry Zeman of Michigan, Tim Renken of Missouri, Norm Strung of Montana, Charles Cornue of Nebraska, Jim Dean of North Carolina, Dale Henegar of North Dakota, Lee Schrimpf of Oklahoma, Nick Sisley of Pennsylvania, Dan Klepper of Texas, Hartt Wixom of Utah, Rex Gerlach of Washington, George Mattis of Wisconsin and Charles Farmer of Wyoming gave me additional information on the status of the true basses in their home states. If the fish are not present in their waters they confirmed the fact.

Half a lifetime of fishing has brought me in contact with many fine anglers. We have fished together, shared campfires and boats, and

iii

swapped fishing tips and fishing stories. The practical side of fishing is developed in this manner, and I am sure my friends will not object to my passing on what I can of this wealth of informally accumulated angling knowledge.

A Bibliography of the Striped Bass or Rockfish produced by the Sport Fishing Institute of Washington, D.C., and technical papers supplied by the Bureau of Sport Fisheries and Wildlife, United States Department of the Interior, have also been helpful in pinpointing the sources to which I could turn for hard-to-get information.

Finally, I am indebted to my wife, Ginny. She is not an angler, but she loves fish on the platter and is an excellent cook. She is also an uncomplaining outdoor gal, and an avid camper and photographer. She has been of help in more ways than I can adequately describe. The index is one of her many contributions to this book.

Bob Gooch

CONTENTS

PREFACE

When measured against an angling career launched several years prior to school age, my introduction to the true basses came well along in life. The size of that first bass did not impress me. It was a little white perch, the smallest member of the bass family—and a tiny one, at that.

That little fish fascinated me though, and so did scores of others I caught that day. All came from what appeared to be a single school. I did not move a dozen feet, but caught many more than I wanted. Most went back into the icy April water.

Four years of college followed immediately by service in World War II interrupted my angling career temporarily, and it was early in the postwar era that a business assignment landed me in Washington, D.C., the Nation's Capital. By then I had resumed my angling pursuits with the same gusto that had marked my early years as an angler. Consequently I was a little let down when fate destined me to life in the big city.

However, while my wife was busy getting acquainted with the many points of interest in the famous city I was trying to locate some half-acceptable fishing water. One of my business associates was an enthusiastic angler and when he learned of my plight he suggested I try the white perch in the Potomac River. It was early April. "They should be running now," he said.

And running they were. My friend had suggested that I try the fishing just below the Chain Bridge, and I persuaded my wife to go with me since it was a sunny day and the weather in the District of Columbia area was warm and balmy. We quickly located the bridge and a glance at the crowd lining both banks of the river told me we were at the right place. Hundreds of happy fishermen of both sexes and of all ages were busy with their angling. And everyone was catching fish.

Ginny and I found a spot on the boulder-strewn shore and I baited light tackle with portions of bloodworms. The water was fast and badly colored, but I caught fish as fast as I could haul them in and rebait my tiny hook. The supply of perch seemed endless.

Those little perch quickly won my respect. They hit hard and readily and fought well in the swift current. Late that evening we dressed a half dozen or so, rolled them in cornmeal and fried them in deep fat. . . . I was hooked for life.

As the spring weeks passed, the run of perch dwindled and finally ended completely. In the meantime I had become a perch fisherman.

After the perch fishing was over, I had the opportunity to meet another member of the true bass family, the big silvery-colored striped bass that also roamed the Potomac as well as nearby Chesapeake Bay. In recent years pollution has taken its toll of the Potomac, but white perch still fight their way through it to the relatively clean waters near the Chain Bridge above the city. Chesapeake Bay also has pollution problems, but the striper is a hardy fish also and still a joy to Bay area anglers.

It was ten years later on big Dale Hollow Reservoir near the Kentucky-Tennessee border that I met the white bass, like the white perch and the striped bass, a flashy silver-toned scrapper. Those exciting school fish strengthened my respect for the true basses. And finally just a year ago I completed my introduction to the family in an exciting encounter with yellow bass on a little lake in the Mississippi Valley.

That is the true bass family—the big striped bass, the tasty little white perch, the slashing white bass, and the golden-hued yellow bass.

Striped bass and white perch are natives of our Atlantic Coast waters —our bays and sounds, tidal rivers and rolling surf. These two basses are anadromous, living in both fresh and salt water, and thriving in both. The white and yellow bass, however, are freshwater fish, natives of the Midwest, the Great Lakes region and the vast Mississippi River drainage system.

Except for the yellow bass, all have been widely introduced. The big striped bass were the first to fin strange waters when they were shipped across country almost a century ago and released in the San Francisco Bay area. The striper is now an established favorite among Pacific Coast surf fishermen. The white bass, too, has been stocked widely in big reservoirs scattered across the southern half of the United States. He bids well to become a mainstay in the big impoundments. The striped bass also shows promise in these reservoirs that so often pose problems for fish management people.

The white perch has been stocked extensively within its natural range and in recent years the littlest bass has turned up in the Great Lakes and as far west as Nebraska. The yellow bass has been introduced to new waters within its range, but little or no effort has been made to expand the range of this locally popular fish.

Generally, the true basses have demonstrated a willingness to accept man's management of their destiny. This plus a reasonable tolerance for less than pure waters points to a bright future for these interesting fish. This should gladden the hearts of anglers everywhere for the true basses are fine sport fish—fun to catch and tasty on the platter.

One of the delightful things about the true basses is the wide variety of angling methods that can be employed to catch them. Take the striped bass, or striper as it is so fondly called, for example. Trolling is probably the most popular method of fishing for them, but even the trollers in recent years have learned the joy of casting to them with light tackle. Consequently, many anglers haul in their heavy tackle and break out light spinning or casting tackle when they hit a school. And in some waters such as East Lake in North Carolina anglers plug for small to medium size stripers in the same manner that they would fish for largemouth bass. Fly fishermen slip into chest waders and work big streamers over grassy flats and surf fishermen use the same waders to protect themselves from the icy ocean waters as they toss heavy surf lures beyond the breakers.

The white perch is a light tackle favorite. Anglers use ultralight spinning tackle and fly rods and catch them on tiny spoons and spinners or colorful streamers. The bloodworm is likely the most popular lure for white perch, but these hardy little bass will hit live minnows as well.

Light spinning tackle probably takes most of the white and yellow bass, but here too light casting tackle or fly rods can be employed. The fly-fisherman may have some difficulty as most white and yellow bass are caught in deep water. The jig or doll fly is a favorite lure for the white bass.

The largemouth and smallmouth bass, those oversized members of the sunfish family, have carved a permanent niche in the history of bass fishing in America. I, for one, am happy to leave it that way. They are fine fighting fish.

The true basses, too, are worthy of the magic word, "bass."

B.G.

Chapter 1

MEET THE BASS FAMILY

I am not about to risk raising the hackles on the backs of thousands of enthusiastic bass anglers across the country by insisting that their prize catches of both large- and smallmouth bass are just oversize sunfish. Nor am I likely to admit that those bronzed battlers that get me out of bed before dawn are anything but smallmouth bass.

But let us face the facts.

The true basses are another breed.

There are four of them in America. Two live in fresh water only, but the other half of the quartet are salt or brackish water fish that spend much of their lives in fresh water.

Let us, for the moment, call them those other bass.

The freshwater purists are the white and yellow basses, *Morone chrysops* and *Morone Mississippiensis,* while the salt or brackish water variety are the striped bass, *Morone Saxatilis,* and the white perch, *Morone Americana.* Most field guides still use *Roccus* instead of *Morone* as the new designation is a recently adopted one. The yellow bass is also often called *Morone interruptus.* All of the true basses are a subfamily of the sea bass family—*Serranidae.*

These four fish are also frequently referred to as the temperate basses.

Because of its size the striped bass is the most popular of the true basses. These handsome fish may live more than 140 years and attain weights of 125 pounds or more, but fish in excess of 75 pounds are rare and their life expectancy is closer to 10 or 12 years. A 125-pound striper is over 5 feet in length. The rod and reel record of 72 pounds was caught in Massachusetts.

The white bass is becoming increasingly popular, and provides many hours of exciting fishing in the Great Lakes and in the big reservoirs across the southern half of the United States. These bass run much smaller and a 3- to 4-pounder is considered a lunker. The world record, a whopping 5-pound, 5-ouncer was caught at Ferguson Lake, Calif., Mar. 8, 1972, by Norman W. Mize.

Both the yellow bass and white perch are smaller fish with 2- and 3-pounders rare. They average less than a pound in weight and under 10 inches in length. The world record white perch, weighing 4 pounds, 12 ounces and measuring 19½ inches in length, was taken from Messalonskee Lake, Maine, on June 4, 1949, by Mrs. Earl Small.

1

(Left) A fine striped bass, a favorite of surf-fishermen along the Atlantic and Pacific Coasts and in many large inland reservoirs. (Right) A white bass from the headwaters of a Tennessee reservoir. A popular fish in the Midwest, Great Lakes and in many big reservoirs.

A common characteristic of all the basses is a dorsal fin deeply notched between the spines and rays. The dorsal spines are graduated in height progressively lower from front to back. The number of rays and spines varies slightly between the species.

All of the basses, except the yellow bass which has a golden overtone, are of a handsome silvery-white color. Black longitudinal lines are another distinguishing feature of the true basses. These lines are very pronounced on the striped, white and yellow basses, but not as much so on the white perch. The white perch does have a long lateral line running along its flanks, and an angler with good vision and a little imagination can put irregular longitudinal lines on most specimens. The lines on the yellow bass are slightly interrupted, a feature that has prompted some fishery men to label the fish *Morone interruptus* instead of *Morone Mississippiensis*. *Mississippiensis* recognizes the yellow bass' natural range in the big Mississippi Valley. The pronounced stripes provide the basis for the striped bass' most common name, and even the white bass is often referred to as the striped bass or striper.

Like most fish, the true basses are the victims of a wide variety of common names. The little yellow bass is often called streaker or black-striped bass because of the stripes down its flanks. It is also called barfish—and sometimes gold bass because of its color. The white bass is probably most often referred to as striper or stripe, but also silver bass, streaker and barfish. Its stripes and silver color are responsible for this designation. The popular striped bass is the most abused. It is frequently called rockfish because of its love for rocky coasts and shorelines. It is also called greenhead, striper, streaked bass, rock and squid hound. The white perch gets by easily—silver perch or sea perch. Chesapeake Bay area anglers call the white perch bluenosed perch or stiffback perch.

All of the basses move around a lot in schools. They eat any kind of animal life of suitable size—with small shrimp, crustaceans, squids, worms and insect larvae providing them with frequent meals. Small fish are a favorite food.

By nature the striped bass is a coastal fish. It prefers inshore waters, bays, and coastal rivers, rocky reefs and sandy beaches. The white bass was originally a fish of the larger rivers and lakes of the Midwest and of the Great Lakes. These popular bass like open water, rarely seeking hiding places. The yellow bass is also a native Midwesterner where it has long been common in the larger rivers, their backwaters, adjoining lakes and major tributaries. The yellow bass likes gravel bars, rocky reefs and underwater brush and vegetation. The white perch, originally a fish of the brackish and tidal waters of the Atlantic Coast, is also now common in many freshwater lakes and ponds.

All of the basses except the yellow bass ascend rivers during the spawning season when possible. The striped bass sometimes goes 75 to 100 miles upstream on its annual spawning runs. Even the landlocked fish follow this spawning instinct, ascending rivers which feed the large reservoirs in which they live. Both the white bass and the white perch also seek the free-flowing waters of feeder streams during the spawning season, though both can spawn successfully in shallow water over

(Top) The little white perch is a favorite of many anglers from Maine to Florida. Photo courtesy of Maine Department of Inland Fisheries and Game. (Bottom) A hybrid bass—cross between a striped bass and white bass. This fish was taken from Cherokee Lake in Tennessee. Photo courtesy of Tennessee Game and Fish Commission.

shoals, rocks or gravel bars. The yellow bass deposits its eggs over gravel bars, rocky reefs or underwater brush or debris.

Generally speaking, the true basses are big-water fish, though both the white perch and yellow bass have been introduced to many small ponds and lakes.

The natural range of the striped bass is the Atlantic Ocean from the St. Lawrence River in Canada to the St. Johns River in Florida and the

(Top to bottom) White bass, striped bass and yellow bass. Photo courtesy of Tennesse Game and Fish Commission.

Gulf Coast from western Florida to Lake Pontchartrain, Louisiana. The big bass are particularly abundant in the Chesapeake Bay and Albemarle Sound. The original range of the white bass was the Mississippi River and the Great Lakes drainage system, while yellow bass were found from Minnesota and Wisconsin south to Alabama and Texas. Like its larger relative, the striped bass, the little white perch was also originally a fish of the Atlantic Coast, though its range was more limited—from Nova Scotia south to the Carolinas.

With the possible exception of the yellow bass, the ranges of all of the basses have been extended by transplanting seed stock to other waters—many of them far from the fish's native home.

The basses have demonstrated that they can adapt to changes in environment and as a result man has not only extended their ranges considerably, but has also introduced them to waters quite different from those with which nature provided them. The fish have shown that they are willing to accept man's management of their destiny.

Early management efforts were directed toward the big striped bass so popular among anglers along the Atlantic Coast. As early as 1879, a tank of 132 little stripers from the Navesink River in New Jersey were hauled across the continent by rail and released in San Francisco Bay. Another release was made in 1882 and California anglers now land approximately 750,000 stripers annually. The migratory fish have spread up and down the West Coast with catches being reported from Mexico to the mouth of the Columbia River. A sizable population lives in Coos Bay, Oregon.

In 1941, a few striped bass were trapped behind the dam when the gates to the big Santee-Cooper Reservoir in South Carolina were closed. By the late '40's anglers were making spectacular catches of the land-locked stripers. South Carolina biologists became interested and soon learned that the normally anadromous fish did not have to return to salt water as a part of their life cycle. A few years later, Virginia biologists established a flourishing striped bass fishery in new Kerr Reservoir on the Roanoke River. Fingerling stripers have since been introduced to big reservoirs throughout the United States, and the fish show promise of becoming a major species of the impoundments.

The white bass too has proven himself a natural for the big reservoirs and has been widely introduced. The fish are very prolific and white bass populations have a habit of exploding in the big lakes, providing fast and interesting fishing.

Forage fish are necessary to the successful establishment of both the striped and white bass in multiple-use impoundments. Both the alewife and gizzard shad meet this need. Like the basses, the shad and alewife are highly prolific and predation is necessary to control their numbers. The true basses provide this service.

Popular within their natural ranges, but somewhat small, the white perch and yellow bass have not been stocked widely beyond their native waters. However, they have been introduced to many new lakes and ponds within their ranges. Many of these releases have been made by anglers and pond owners rather than by professional fishery men.

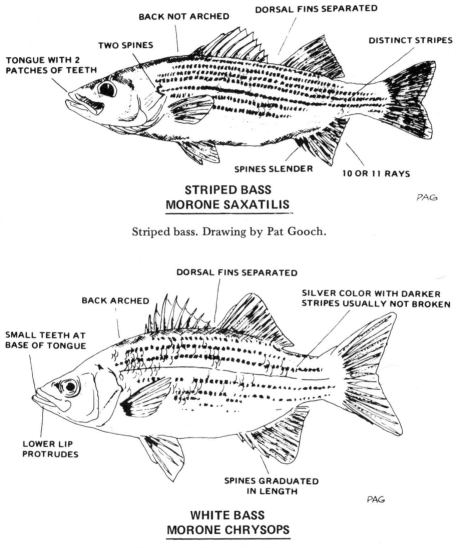

Striped bass. Drawing by Pat Gooch.

Experimental stockings of white perch have been made as far west as Nebraska. The yellow bass has not demonstrated a willingness to adapt readily to artificial impoundments as has its relative, the white bass.

All of the basses take artificial lures readily, and hit hard with gritty determination. They are not acrobatic, and seldom put on an aerial show, but they roll on the surface, make long and determined runs and slug it out in the depths. Even the little white perch rarely disappoints the angler.

The true basses are school fish, and this gives them added angling appeal—for once the angler lands a fish he can be reasonably sure there are others around. When he determines what they are hitting and the depth at which they are feeding he can anticipate some fast fishing.

With most of the fish running small (a pound or two, at the most), light tackle adds considerably to the thrill of fishing for white perch and for both the white and yellow bass. For the most part, however, heavier tackle is indicated for the larger striped bass, though these fish too may run small in certain waters. When they do they too provide exciting fishing on light tackle. Spinning tackle probably takes most of the bass caught in this country, though some anglers prefer fly rods or even light bait-casting tackle.

Choose your tackle and you will find a member of the bass family ready to take you on.

Probably the bulk of the striped bass caught in the United States and Canada are taken by trolling methods. Anglers operate from small charter boats and private yachts or outboards. Charter boats capable of fishing a party of three to five anglers are very popular in the Chesapeake Bay and other waters in which the big bass abound.

Of course, the striper has long been a favorite of the hardy surf-fishing clan. Standing knee-deep in the surging surf, and casting heavy lures beyond the breakers along a wave-tossed beach is a heady experience that many anglers will swear surpasses all forms of angling. The trollers are probably more successful, but I imagine the dedicated surf-fisherman could care less.

Fly-fishermen wade the flats and work popping bugs over schools of feeding stripers, and in some parts of their range, plug casters fish for them in much the same manner as they would for largemouth bass. Bait-fishermen drift soft-shell crabs to hungry stripers.

Probably the most popular method of fishing for white bass is to cruise slowly about a lake watching for "jumps." The "jumps" occur when the schools of bass discover a school of shad and tear into it, creating quite a disturbance as the frantic little fish skip over the surface in an effort to escape. The angler then moves in and casts to the school until it sounds. He then looks for another school. Light spinning tackle is ideal for this kind of fishing.

When the bass are not feeding on the surface the angler must resort to fishing deep, trolling spinners or small lures in channels, bays, or over sandbars, or fishing near the bottom with small live minnows. During the summer months night fishing is popular.

Another popular method of fishing for white bass is employed in the spring as they make their spawning runs up feeder streams. Anglers line the banks or fish from boats, casting small lures or fishing with live bait.

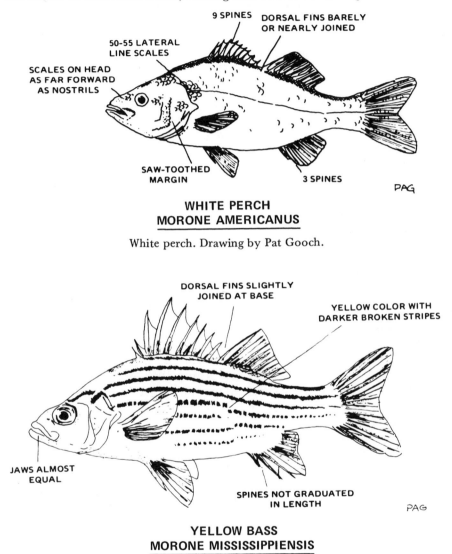

WHITE PERCH
MORONE AMERICANUS

White perch. Drawing by Pat Gooch.

YELLOW BASS
MORONE MISSISSIPPIENSIS

Yellow bass. Drawing by Pat Gooch.

Most yellow bass are caught on live baits such as minnows, garden worms and night crawlers. Cut baits are also popular. Trolling near the bottom with spinner-bait or spinner-fly combinations is often productive. When the yellow bass move into the shallows, spinners, spoons, flies and popping bugs are productive. They provide exciting fishing.

Worms are probably the bait most frequently used in fishing for tasty white perch. Like the white bass, they make spawning runs in the spring, and when they do the fishing can be fast and interesting in tributary streams, shallow coves or river estuaries. When the temperature hits 60º F. the little bass seek out a tributary stream in which to spawn.

Probably the next most popular method is casting tiny spoons and lures with light spinning tackle. The little bass hit hard and fight well on light tackle.

Fly-fishing enthusiasts catch white perch on small streamers and spinner-fly combinations, and watch for late evening rises when the perch dimple the surface and suck in small insects. This is dry-fly time —and rare sport while it lasts. The white perch holds an edge over the other basses in being a favorite of ice-fishermen.

The white and striped bass have long been popular market fish and so their food value is well established. Their meat is white and flaky and very tasty. The firm, succulent meat of the white perch is delightful on the platter and in the spring, perch roe dipped in flour and eggs and quickly browned makes a rare feast. The flesh of the yellow bass is also white and flaky, and delicious when pan or deep-fat fried.

While both the white and yellow basses are relatively short-lived, they are very prolific, laying up to half a million eggs at spawning time. Most white bass die before they are four years old, and very few yellow bass live longer than five years. Both the white perch and striped bass lead longer lives—up to 12 to 15 years, with some healthy fish exceeding that life span. They too are prolific.

The striped and white basses have been raised successfully in hatcheries and have proven themselves adaptable to life in the big impoundments. These basses have been successfully crossbred, developing an interesting hybrid.

All things considered, the true basses could well become the bass of the future. They have already staked out a strong claim to a share of American angling. That share is not likely to diminish. Given time, they may well challenge the large- and smallmouth bass to their just claim as the basses of America.

Chapter 2

THE WORLD OF THE BASSES

The waters of the Atlantic Ocean off the coast of New England are cold—even in June. However, the eager angler, standing knee-deep in the foaming surf, is dressed for it. Roomy chest waders blanket his body from the armpits down. The only other visible clothing is a heavy wool shirt, tucked into the waders, and a broad-brimmed fishing hat that protects his face and neck. The chances of the mild swells crashing over those waders are slight, and if the angler should fall, a broad belt around his midriff will keep most of the water out of his boots.

The belt also serves other purposes. A sturdy gaff dangles from it—handy to the angler's left hand. There is also a small lure box and a sheath knife for cutting bait.

Behind the angler on the sandy Cape Cod beach is the rest of his gear. Most of it is neatly arranged in his self-styled beach buggy, a four-wheel-drive automobile fitted with big balloon tires for negotiating the soft sand. A long sand spike rests in the sand, leaning slightly toward the rolling ocean, and beside it is a comfortable beach chair. The periods of fast action are separated by long dull ones, and the chair gives him a chance to relax, his long rod resting in the sand spike and a heavy pyramid sinker holding his baited hook out where a feeding fish might discover it.

The angler's fishing tackle consists of a long glass rod and a heavy saltwater spinning reel, the kind of equipment fast gaining converts among those who fish America's many miles of surf.

Our angler is a surf-fisherman. He is working the Cape Cod surf for one of America's favorite fish, the handsome silver-colored striped bass that frequent the New England coast in June.

Let us shift the scene across the continent. A similarly outfitted western angler stands braced against the strong Pacific swells. Here too the beach is sandy, but huge boulders protrude through the sand and dot the foaming surf. And behind the angler a rugged boulder-bolstered coastline reaches high toward a blue western sky.

The western angler is also fishing for striped bass, the same fish our Cape Cod man is working so hard to catch. But these are transplanted stripers (transplanted from the Atlantic waters the eastern angler is fishing but a few miles to the south in New Jersey).

Now swing back east to the Low Country of South Carolina. The month is May and a pair of veteran anglers are trolling big Santee-

Cooper Reservoir in a broad-beamed outboard boat. A couple of 20-inch stripers lay gleaming in the bottom of their boat, but there are bigger fish in the huge impoundment. The anglers are not likely to be satisfied until they land one.

These fish are striped bass, too, but they are landlocked in the fresh water of the big reservoir. The fish fare well in this strange environment and anglers travel for miles to troll or cast for the landlocked stripers.

Due north from Santee-Cooper, straddling the North Carolina-Virginia border, lies big Kerr Reservoir—or Buggs Island Lake, as Virginians call it. Here, too, anglers troll for landlocked stripers. The story is the same; just the actors are different.

Striped bass anglers on Chesapeake Bay.

Kerr Reservoir straddles the Roanoke River, long a top striped bass stream. When the lake was formed, Virginia fishery managers, envious of the success of their South Carolina colleagues, set about establishing their own landlocked striped bass fishery. Their efforts were quickly justified. Today, Virginia and North Carolina anglers fish for striped bass in the turbulent waters below the huge dam, troll for them in the big lake, and float the major tributary streams that feed the lake, casting for the spawning fish as they move up the Dan and Roanoke Rivers on their April and May spawning runs.

Now let us move north again—to the Chesapeake Bay in Maryland and Virginia. Experts say the big Chesapeake Bay is the major breeding ground for the Atlantic striped bass fishery.

Here, too, trolling is popular. A typical autumn Saturday morning will bring forth dozens of small charter boats, capable of fishing four or five anglers; and scores of private boats. Most troll the broad waters of the Bay for striped bass, or rocks, as they are fondly referred to in this prime striped bass country. Some anglers prefer to move into the shallow areas, then anchor or beach their boats and cast to the bass with bucktail lures or spoons. They catch pan-size stripers, fun to do battle with and delicious on the platter.

This exciting fishing occurs all up and down the Atlantic Coast—in tiny Delaware, New Jersey, Long Island Sound, in the prime waters of little Rhode Island and along the rocky coast of Maine.

These fishing scenes are all set within the natural range of the striped bass. However, the bass' original range has been extended considerably by transplanting. The advent of landlocked striped bass in Santee-Cooper and Kerr Reservoirs was not an expansion of the striper's range for the fish were already there. Stripers, on their annual spawning runs, were already making extensive use of the rivers which feed these impoundments. They were simply trapped behind the dams when they were closed.

However, the successful establishment of the anadromous fish in these freshwater lakes encouraged fishery managers in other states to try them in their own waters. Fingerling bass from North and South Carolina and Virginia have since gone west to Tennessee, Kentucky, Oklahoma, Arizona and other states far from the briny waters. As of this writing, striped bass fishing in these new areas is mostly in the experimental stages, but the picture is encouraging. Stripers, like the white bass, appear adaptable to life in the big reservoirs that are changing the landscape throughout so much of America.

The striped bass is an anadromous fish of the Atlantic Ocean drainages from the St. Lawrence River in Canada to the St. Johns River in Florida and of the Gulf of Mexico river drainages from Florida to Louisiana. Some trophy fish are taken in Nova Scotia and along the Maine Coast.

The major river drainages along the Atlantic Coast include the Hudson River in New York, the Delaware River, the Chesapeake Bay into which flow the Susquehanna, Potomac, Rappahannock and James Rivers, Albemarle Sound and the Roanoke River which forms Kerr Reservoir, Cooper River in South Carolina, a part of the Santee-Cooper complex, and the St. Johns River in Florida.

Along the Gulf of Mexico coast, the Apalachicola and Alabama River systems are the major striped bass spawning rivers.

Yearling stripers were introduced to the Pacific Coast in 1879 and 1881 and the fish are now just as popular among West Coast anglers as they are in the East. The best fishing is along the California coast, particularly in the San Francisco Bay area, but the fish range the Pacific coastal waters from Mexico to the mouth of the Columbia River.

High in the Great Smoky Mountains of North Carolina, a Fontana Lake angler cruises slowly along the winding shoreline of the mountain reservoir. He is not fishing, but a light spinning rod and open-face reel rest convenient to his casting arm. A small spoon dangles from the end of his light monofilament line. He is ready to go into action on a moment's notice. It is August and even at the high altitude of Fontana Village, the summer heat is noticeable. The sun shimmers off the smooth surface of the blue water and the angler squints as his eyes sweep back and forth.

A fine catch of New Mexico white bass. Photo courtesy of New Mexico Department of Game and Fish.

Suddenly the angler straightens from his slumped position and spins the boat to his left. A surface disturbance near the center of the lake attracts his attention. He revs the motor and the boat shoots ahead. The surface is fairly boiling now and he cuts the motor as the boat drifts quietly within casting range of the fracas.

His first cast brings a jolting strike; so does the next—and the next. He does not waste time playing the fish that average a pound to a pound and a half. There is not enough time. As he unhooks his third fish, the surface commotion ends suddenly, the school sounds and the few moments of fast fishing are over.

The angler is neither surprised nor disappointed. He strings his catch, guns his motor and starts looking for another school of bass.

White bass anglers camped on a feeder stream of a western white bass reservoir.

This is white bass fishing as it is practiced during the summer vacation months on the big multiple-use reservoirs across the South and Midwest. The nomadic bass roam in search of minnows. When they find a school they go into a frenzy, gobbling up the frantic little fish until those that are left get untracked and escape. The bass are then off in search of another school.

This is "fishing the jumps," as it is commonly referred to. The frantic little fish scramble and jump in an attempt to escape the slashing white bass.

The white bass is not native to the majority of the reservoirs he thrives in, but like his larger cousin, the striped bass, he has adapted to life in the impoundments and promises to become a mainstay in these big fishing waters.

It is April and spring is making a strong bid along the major tributary of a big reservoir in Kentucky. The weather is still cold and a raw wind keeps the less hardy indoors, but the dozen or so anglers lining the

A fine hybrid bass taken in Tennessee. Photo courtesy of Tennessee Game and Fish Commission.

banks of the stream or wading the shallows are not about to seek the warmth of a fireside. Not yet, at least. The white bass are running—heading up the big tributary stream on their annual spawning migration. A few anglers have already loaded their stringers and returned to their cars to warm themselves while waiting for companions to fill their own limits.

Switch the spotlight to Lake Erie and the Kelley Island section of this large natural lake. A pair of anglers in an anchored boat are working the water around a small island. Periodically, one or the other snaps his casting arm upward, sets the hook, and plays a flashing, silver-colored fish to the boat. The fishermen are working a school of white bass feeding in their native waters. The popular white bass is native to Lake Erie where it was once an important commercial fish. They were once so numerous that commercial fishermen glutted the market. Tons of white bass were thrown away.

The Bass Islands section of Lake Erie is another popular Great Lakes fishing area, and the fish still provides many happy hours of angling for those who appreciate him.

Let us go back south to winding Claytor Lake on the New River in Virginia. Here, anglers fish the spawning run in the spring and the

(Left) A lone angler casts for white bass in Holston River, Tennessee. (Right) White bass caught in June in the island region of Lake Erie. Photo courtesy of Ohio Department of Natural Resources.

"jumps" during the summer months, but there is still another bass fishing attraction. The month is July. Many local anglers prefer to fish after dark when the temperature on the lake is more inviting. A pair of anglers run their boat to a white bass hotspot, anchor and hang a couple of gasoline lanterns over the water. They bait up with lively one-inch-long minnows and lower their hook about 20 feet in the quiet water of the mountain reservoir. They settle back for action; it is not long coming.

The angler in the bow of the boat straightens from a slumped position, takes up the slack in his line, and with a flick of his wrist sets the hook. The fish reacts violently and the fight is joined. It ends quickly however, and the angler in the stern swings a big boat net over the side and lifts his buddy's catch aboard.

Night fishing is popular on many southern reservoirs during the hot summer months. The gasoline lantern attracts insects. Many fall on the water and they in turn attract small fish. The white bass moves in to feed on the little fish. A legalized form of baiting!

The white bass was originally a fish of the Mississippi River drainage system from the Great Lakes to the Gulf of Mexico. This big chunk of country holds many acres of water in the heart of America and the white bass is no stranger to anglers throughout this vast region. However, its introduction to waters far beyond its natural range may well have made the little bass more popular in other parts of the country.

In many parts of the South and Southwest the bass' presence went almost unnoticed until the impoundment of many of these streams by the U.S. Army Corps of Engineers, the Tennessee Valley Authority and major power companies. The white bass populations seemed to explode in these big impoundments, creating fast and interesting fishing.

The white bass has also become a favorite fish for experimental stocking, with transplants being made in such faraway states as Florida, Colorado and even California. They have also been introduced to many lakes draining into the Atlantic Ocean.

Spring is in the air and city-bound anglers in the District of Columbia can no longer resist the urge that for ages has drawn man to lakes and streams at this season of the year.

The word goes out that the white perch are running!

No true angler in the Washington, D.C., area needs additional information. He simply assembles his tackle, buys a package of bloodworms and heads for the Potomac—or more specifically the Chain Bridge area of that famous river. He will join (or be joined by) hundreds of other anglers. They include men, women and children equipped with cane poles, fly rods, light spinning tackle, bait-casting outfits and completely inappropriate saltwater trolling tackle! It makes no difference. They will all catch fish and the fellow with the cane pole will enjoy his outing just as much as the man more ideally outfitted with spinning tackle.

White perch in untold numbers head up the Potomac every spring on their annual search for ideal spawning grounds. Apparently many are successful, for the mighty Potomac offers good white perch fishing from spring to fall and from the fall line at Washington, D.C., to the Chesapeake Bay.

At about the same time a hundred odd miles south in the broad Back Bay of Virginia, better known for its largemouth bass fishing, a lone angler in a weathered boat cranks up his outboard and heads for a protected cove. He too is on his way to fish for white perch, or "stiffback" perch. And he is likely to fill the small galvanized tub in the bow of his boat. There is no limit on white perch in Virginia. Biologists say the fishing would be better if more of the prolific fish were taken from the Potomac River, Back Bay and other good perch waters.

Surf fishing for striped bass in the Virginia Beach surf.

Several hundred miles up the Atlantic Coast on a picturesque little peninsula of sand known as Cape Cod, a lone angler runs a thin wire hook through the lips of a lively minnow, adjusts his red and white bobber about three feet above the hook, and softly casts the rig to the edge of an aquatic grass patch about ten feet from his boat. He watches the bobber settle on the water and then dance merrily as the minnow frisks about. Grunting his satisfaction, he lights a battered pipe and settles back to relax and wait.

This angler is fishing for chain pickerel. The sparkling Cape Cod pond is full of the long-snouted fish, but few anglers fish for them.

Suddenly the bouncing bobber picks up a new beat, dances vigorously and disappears. Pickerel fisherman that he is, the angler waits for it to bob back to the surface, but it does not do so. This is the angler's cue that something other than a pickerel is on the end of his line. He lifts his rod tip, reels in the slack line—and strikes! His slender rod develops a rainbow curve and he plays his fish carefully. There is no surface-cracking leap, no flashy fighting—just stubborn resistance deep in the blue water.

Carefully, the angler works his catch to the side of the boat and slips the net under a glistening silver-hued white perch. It is a good fish— almost 12 inches long.

The angler is elated, even though his catch is not a pickerel. There are many good white perch waters among the freshwater ponds on Cape Cod, and some of the fish grow to good size, probably as large as they do anywhere.

Back on the mainland and still farther north, the sun is setting as an angler boards a small rowboat at the dock on a peaceful Maine lake. There is no motor on his boat. He does not have far to go, and wants to avoid spooking a school of fish feeding on the surface in a nearby cove.

The gentle ripples from countless small dimples collide with each other as he moves into range with his light fly rod. There is no breeze. He does not drop an anchor.

The boat drifts slowly as he works out a long line and drops a tiny dry fly on the calm surface. He is quickly in business as the fish slurp up his offering. The willowy fly rod lets him enjoy every move of the fighting fish as he works it to the boat. A fat white perch goes into the fish box, and the angler is soon playing another one.

White perch often feed on the surface of these Maine lakes as darkness settles over the north country. They provide interesting fishing on light fly tackle.

The white perch, like its big cousin, the striped bass, is an anadromous fish living in the Atlantic coastal waters from Nova Scotia south to the Carolinas. Most salt or brackish waters that hold white perch are also likely to harbor a few striped bass. Those same Atlantic drainage systems listed for striped bass are good bets for white perch fishing, though the perch's range is not as extensive. They are not found along the Gulf of Mexico coast.

In recent years the white perch has invaded Lake Erie. Perch are often found landlocked in freshwater lakes and ponds. Because of the lack of widespread angler interest in the usually small white perch, there has been very little introduction of the species to new waters beyond its range. However, anglers seem to be showing a new appreciation for the littlest bass and this attitude could well change. In recent years white perch have been stocked in new waters as far west as Nebraska.

"The bass are hitting." These are magic words along the big river towns in Illinois. And it is neither the largemouth nor smallmouth bass that creates all the excitement. It could be white bass, but chances are good that the little yellow bass is the fish of the hour.

A lucky angler and his guide admire a nice landlocked striper taken from Santee-Cooper Reservoirs in South Carolina.

These bright yellow members of the true bass family are not as widespread as the other basses and consequently do not enjoy as much popularity as their cousins. However, within its range the yellow bass is a favorite among anglers.

The range of the yellow bass is from southern Minnesota, Wisconsin, and Iowa south to Texas and Louisiana. The fish is particularly abundant in the Mississippi Valley, and like the white bass, is primarily a fish of the Mississippi River drainage system.

The yellow bass prefers large rivers and lakes and is most abundant in the northern reaches of its range. At Lake Chautauqua near Havana,

Illinois, the yellow bass may make up as much as 30 percent of the total angling catch.

In parts of its range the yellow bass may receive little or no attention from anglers. This is probably due to the fact that the fish is not always abundant in the smaller streams and lakes where it occurs.

While there has been limited transplanting of yellow bass within its natural range, this has been primarily the work of private pond or lake owners who want to introduce the fish to their waters. Little or no effort has been made to expand the natural range of the yellow bass. Possibly, interest in the white and striped bass, and the success of these stocking programs may spill over to the yellow bass some day. If and when it does, the colorful little bass is likely to become an angling favorite also.

The world of the true basses, like that of the fish themselves, is varied and interesting. And the best thing about this world is that it is expanding, and the fish are gaining new friends as they adapt to new waters—often far from their native ones.

Chapter 3

THE BASS STATES

Of the 50 states that make up this great nation, 44 report the presence of one or more of the true basses in their waters. Several of the states which do not have this kind of fishing are studying the possibility of introducing the white or striped bass, or both. Most interest centers upon the big striped bass, a handsome fish, very popular wherever it is found.

This chapter is based upon the results of a survey made especially for this book. The information was gathered from the fish or conservation departments of the several states, and in most instances, also, from data supplied by fellow outdoor writers based in the respective states.

For the angler who wants to develop additional information from a particular state I am also listing the appropriate state agency that can furnish additional information on fishing for the true basses.

Alabama

Three members of the true bass family fin the waters of Alabama. Present are the striped bass, white bass, and yellow bass. All are native to this popular fishing state deep in the heart of Dixie.

A few striped bass continue to enter the Mobile Delta; however, the spawning runs up the Coosa and Tallapoosa Rivers have been reduced drastically during the past 10 years. Striped bass have been introduced to the major rivers of the Mobile Bay drainages in an effort to reestablish strong spawning runs. At present the best striper fishing is found in Lake Martin on the Tallapoosa River and in Lakes Jordan, Lay and Mitchell on the Coosa River. The state record for striped bass is 55 pounds.

Both the white and yellow bass are present in the Mobile Bay drainages and in the Tennessee River. Both are native to these waters. The white bass has been introduced to several impoundments and stream drainages throughout the state. The state record white bass, a 3-pound, 10-ouncer, came from Lake Smith. The fish were introduced to this impoundment and it has become one of the top white bass waters in Alabama.

Apparently the striped and white bass have bright futures in Alabama as they are introduced to new waters. The yellow bass is abundant in the Tennessee River, but because of its small size does not receive much attention from fishermen.

The best fishing for all three fish occurs in the spring at the mouths of tributary streams and in the streams themselves as the fish make their spawning runs. The tailraces of the many dams throughout the state provide top fishing in both spring and fall. During the summer months anglers fish the "jumps" in Smith Lake and other impoundments.

The bass seasons are open all year.

Striped bass have been reproduced at hatcheries of the Division of Game and Fish.

State of Alabama
Department of Conservation
Division of Game and Fish
64 North Union Street
Montgomery, Alabama 36104

Alaska

There are no bass in the "Land of the Midnight Sun," but plenty of grayling, salmon and trout. There is little likelihood that any of the true basses will ever be introduced to the 49th state.

State of Alaska
Department of Fish and Game
Subport Building
Juneau, Alaska 99801

Arizona

Both the white and yellow bass and striped bass are found in Arizona waters. There are no white perch. Local anglers refer to the little yellow bass as "stripes." None of the fish are native to this southwestern state, but all have been introduced with varying degrees of success. Stripers have been reproduced in the hatcheries of the Arizona Game and Fish Department.

Fishing for all three basses is legal all year, but the best fishing periods vary between species. The best white bass fishing comes in the spring, while the striped bass fishing hits its peak a few weeks later in early summer. The yellow bass seem to hit equally well in spring and summer. The creel limit for striped bass is three and the minimum size limit is 16 inches.

The best striped bass fishing is found in the Colorado River between Lakes Mohave and Havasu. Yellow bass fishing is good in Canyon and Saguaro Lakes, and Lake Pleasant provides good white bass fishing.

Striped bass fishing promises to continue good and also popular. The present state record of 38 pounds, 12 ounces, came from the Colorado River. The little yellow bass grow to 6–10 inches and are proving themselves interesting panfish. The record of 1 pound, 1 ounce came from Saguaro Lake.

A pair of fine landlocked stripers taken from an Arizona reservoir. Photo courtesy of Arizona Game and Fish Department.

State of Arizona
Game and Fish Department
2222 West Greenway Road
Phoenix, Arizona 85023

Arkansas

Both the white and yellow bass are native to Arkansas, and the striped bass has been introduced. All three are popular among anglers of the state.

The Game and Fish Commission pays little or no attention to the yellow bass, but the little bass fares well on its own. The white bass is a native of the larger rivers in the state and of the old river lakes. However, the fish are netted from time to time and transferred from one lake to another as the situation dictates.

The large, clear, man-made lakes are now producing the best growth among the basses and as a result provide the best fishing.

Both adult and fingerling striped bass have been purchased from the coastal states of North Carolina, South Carolina and Virginia and introduced to suitable Arkansas waters. Many of the fingerlings are held in rearing ponds until they reach 4—6 inches in length.

A 12-pound striped bass holds the state record and the record white bass was checked in at 4 pounds, 15 ounces—a good white bass in any angler's creel.

Most anglers prefer to fish the spring spawning runs for white and yellow bass. However, "jump" fishing is popular later in the year when the shad school in open water.

State of Arkansas
Arkansas Game and Fish Commission
Little Rock, Arkansas 72201

California

The striped bass is abundant in California, but the white bass, a relative newcomer, shows promise in several of the large reservoirs.

Neither of the basses is native to California, though the striped bass was finning Pacific coastal waters long before the ancestors of first and second generation anglers took up residence in the big western state. It was in 1879 that 132 small bass were taken from the Navesink River in New Jersey, and hauled by rail to California and released near Martinez. In 1882, another 300 bass were shipped across the continent and stocked in lower Suisun Bay. Within a decade striped bass were being sold in San Francisco markets. The commercial catch eventually grew to well over a million pounds annually, but in 1935 all commercial fishing was stopped in favor of sport fishery.

In recent years striped bass have been introduced to Millerton Reservoir and to the Lower Colorado River. Some reproduction has taken place in both waters, but a significant fishery has not yet developed.

It was not until 1965 that the white bass was introduced to California waters. However, the fish have established themselves in Nacimiento Lake and anglers are taking them in increasing numbers. This is the first time white bass have been stocked in a California reservoir, but the venture has proven a successful one.

The California record for striped bass was established in 1938 when a 62-pounder was entered in the official record books. Reports of a 65-pound striper taken in 1951 were never verified. The state record white bass, weighing 5-pounds, 5-ounces, was taken in 1972.

Unlike eastern striper fishing, striped bass fishing in California is good all year. However, the fall months are considered the best. White bass fishing excels in the spring months and again in mid-October.

Striped bass are found all along the California coast, but the best fishing is found in the San Francisco Bay and Delta. Nacimiento Lake in San Luis Obispo County is considered the top white bass water in the state.

California fish biologists feel the striped bass populations may suffer from increased fishing pressure in the rapidly growing state, but they are more concerned about demands to develop the estuaries. The white bass, a proven fish of the reservoirs, seems to have a very bright future in California.

> State of California
> Department of Fish and Game
> 1416 Ninth Street
> Sacramento, California 95814

Colorado

Of the four basses in America, only the white bass is found in the high country of Colorado. These fish were first introduced in 1951 and many Colorado anglers have learned to appreciate the silver-colored bass from the Midwest.

A 2-pound, 14-ounce white bass from Bonny Reservoir holds the state record. This fine fish was caught in 1969.

The white bass season never closes in Colorado, but the best fishing occurs in the spring and fall. At the present Adobe, Bonny and Sterling Creek Reservoirs are prime bass waters but the fish are being stocked in suitable impoundments all over the state.

Fishery biologists in Colorado were attracted to the white bass in their search for a predatory fish to contain forage and rough fish in warm-water reservoirs. Efforts to establish the largemouth bass had failed in some waters because the environmental conditions did not favor these fish. The white bass has filled the void in many bodies of water. However, the fishery men have also learned that the white bass spawn successfully only in those reservoirs into which there is a yearly inflow of fresh water during June or July.

> State of Colorado
> Division of Game, Fish and Parks
> Colorado Department of Natural Resources
> 6060 Broadway
> Denver, Colorado 80216

Connecticut

This New England state on the Atlantic rests right in the middle of good white perch and striped bass country. Both fish are native to the state and very abundant. Anglers seek them avidly. Striped bass in the

40 to 50-pound class are taken every season and occasional fish nudge the 60-pound mark.

While these members of the bass family are primarily marine fish in Connecticut, white perch do occur in many freshwater ponds where they expand rapidly and quickly become stunted.

White perch and striped bass fishing is centered around Long Island Sound and its tributaries.

Fishing is legal all year in Connecticut, and there is probably not a month in the year that a few anglers are not out in search of either stripers or perch.

> State of Connecticut
> Board of Fisheries and Game
> State Office Building
> Hartford, Connecticut 06115

Delaware

Both the striped bass and white perch are abundant and popular in this small state on the Atlantic seaboard. The fish are native to the state and found generally throughout the varied waters of Delaware.

New records for both striped bass and white perch were established in 1970. The new bass record was 39 pounds and the record perch weighed 1 pound, 13 ounces.

Fishing for both bass and perch is permitted all year, but the best fishing occurs in the spring and fall. The outlook for both species is good if pollution can be held in check.

Delaware Bay and Indian River Inlet are considered good striped bass waters. These waters are also good for white perch, though the white perch is fairly common throughout the state. Moores Lake and Courseys Pond are good white perch waters.

Bloodworms are a favorite bait for both bass and perch.

> State of Delaware
> Department of Natural Resources
>   and Environmental Control
> Division of Fish and Wildlife
> Dover, Delaware 19901

Florida

The striped bass is the only member of the true bass found to any extent in Florida, a state that prizes its largemouth bass fishing. However, a limited population of white bass is found in the Apalachicola watershed.

While there are no official state records for striped bass, fish upwards of 30 pounds have been taken from native populations. The striped bass is a highly regarded fish in Florida, though the present fishery is mostly limited to the Apalachicola and St. Johns Rivers.

There are no closed fishing seasons in Florida waters, but fishing success is highest during the spring spawning run—March and April.

Striped bass have been successfully introduced to Lakes Bentley, Hunter, Julianna, Newnans, Parker, Talquin and Underhill. The Talquin and Underhill populations show the most promise.

A pair of Florida stripers. Photo courtesy of Florida Game and Freshwater Fish Commission.

Florida has an agreement with the state of South Carolina by which it secures 1,000,000 recently hatched fry annually for its hatchery program. They are held to stockable sizes, 2—4 inches, and released in suitable freshwater lakes.

State of Florida
Game and Fresh Water Fish Commission
Farris Bryant Building
Tallahassee, Florida 32304

Georgia

The striped bass is native to the coastal streams of Georgia and the white bass has been introduced to the major reservoirs. The state fishery people have also experienced some success with "white rock," a hybridization of the striped bass and white bass. The hybrid was developed in South Carolina, but has been stocked in Georgia and is considered an excellent game fish.

Landlocked striped bass are also being introduced to some of the larger reservoirs in the state. This program holds promise and will no doubt be continued.

A 63-pound striped bass holds the present state record. The record white bass, a lunker 4-pound, 15-ouncer, was taken on March 31, 1969, from Lake Lanier.

Bill Baab, Outdoor Editor of the *Augusta Chronicle,* likes the spring, summer and fall months for striped bass. He particularly likes to fish the spawning runs. Bill says white bass can be caught all year in the big reservoirs. April and May are considered good months for both species.

At present, the best striped bass fishing occurs in the major Georgia Rivers—Ocmulgee, Ogeechee and the Savannah, for example. Clark Hill and other big reservoirs are all good white bass waters.

> State of Georgia
> State Game and Fish Commission
> 270 Washington Street, SW
> Atlanta, Georgia 30334

Hawaii

Kenji Ego, Chief of the Fisheries Branch of the Hawaii Division of Fish and Game, reports there are no true basses in our 50th state. He adds that there are no present plans to introduce them.

> State of Hawaii
> Department of Land and
>   Natural Resources
> Division of Fish and Game
> 530 South Hotel Street
> Honolulu, Hawaii 96813

Idaho

Martel Morache of the Idaho Fish and Game Department, says there are no true basses in the waters of his state, and at present there are no plans to introduce them.

> State of Idaho
> Idaho Fish and Game Department
> P.O. Box 25
> 600 South Walnut Street
> Boise, Idaho 83707

Illinois

"Whenever the intriguing words, 'the bass are hitting,' are casually

mentioned at a local sportshop, tavern, barbershop, or wherever fishermen are congregated, many sportsmen normally think of the largemouth or smallmouth bass. Around the big river towns, the speaker
might be questioned and asked to be more specific—what bass? The
truth of the matter is, the gentlemen might be referring to the white
bass or yellow bass rather than the largemouth or smallmouth bass. If
the former is the case, this fellow is probably a member of the devoted
clan of striper and bass fishermen who have experienced many enjoyable hours catching these sporty fishes."

So reads the introductory paragraph of a paper on the true basses of
Illinois by Arnold W. Fritz.

It goes without saying that these two fish are extremely popular in
the "Land of Lincoln." In fact, the little yellow bass may well enjoy its
greatest popularity there.

Both fish are found in abundance in the larger rivers such as the
Illinois and Mississippi. They also occur in some of the natural lakes in
northeastern Illinois.

Both of these members of the true bass family are native to the state
and there has been very little introduction of the fish to new waters.
River pollution is the major problem faced by biologists of the Department of Conservation.

Spring and fall are considered the best fishing periods with the spring
months probably a bit better than the autumn ones. Fishing is legal all
year, however, and a few fish are caught throughout the spring, summer
and fall.

Lake Chautauqua is one of the best yellow bass lakes in the state.
The Fox Chain O'Lakes are considered good for white bass. The yellow
bass is found in many farm ponds, city reservoirs and large artificial
impoundments.

State of Illinois
Department of Conservation
106 State Office Building
400 South Spring Street
Springfield, Illinois 62706

Indiana

As is the situation in Illinois, both the white and yellow bass are
found in the "Hoosier State." They are native to the area, and particularly abundant in the Ohio River watershed.

Lake Freeman is considered one of the top bass waters in Indiana.

Anglers like to fish for the white bass, but do not regard it highly as a
table fish. However, with the construction of a number of large reservoirs in the state, the white bass will no doubt be introduced to new
waters. This may improve the fish's image as a food fish as the waters of

the reservoirs are generally considered cleaner than those of rivers, so many of which are suffering from pollution or other drainage problems which affect the taste of fish.

To date no attempt has been made to hatchery-produce the basses, but sexually mature fish have been purchased for stocking in several small impoundments.

A 4-pound, 3-ounce white bass taken in Carroll County in 1965 holds the present white bass record.

There are no closed seasons on white or yellow bass, but April and May are considered the top fishing months. The creel limit on the true basses is six per day.

> State of Indiana
> Division of Fish and Game
> Indiana Department of Natural Resources
> Room 607 State Office Building
> Indianapolis, Indiana 46204

Iowa

Both the white and yellow bass are found in Iowa, but at the present there is very little angling interest for these two fish. Both species are native to the state.

Clear and Spirit Lakes are both good bass lakes, and a few anglers fish for them in the spring.

> State of Iowa
> Iowa Conservation Commission
> 300 Fourth Street
> Des Moines, Iowa 50319

Kansas

The white bass is an established favorite among the anglers who fish the state's big reservoirs. These fish are native to Kansas, but it was not until the big impoundments were built that the fish realized their full potential.

Spring is the most popular time to fish for white bass, though the season is open all year.

Kanapolis is one of the most popular white bass lakes in the state, but there are several others. The future of white bass fishing seems almost unlimited in this big Midwestern state.

A 5-pound, 4-ounce white bass caught at Topeka, Kansas, on May 4, 1966, by Henry A. Baker, set a new world record. The prize fish measured 17 inches in length.

> State of Kansas
> Kansas Forestry, Fish and
>   Game Department
> Box F
> Pratt, Kansas 67124

Kentucky

Both the white and yellow bass are native to the "Bluegrass State," and the striped bass has been introduced. Only the white perch is absent. White bass are found all over the state in the larger rivers and big impoundments. Yellow bass are found in the western part of the state only—in Barkley and Kentucky Lakes and in the Mississippi and Ohio Rivers.

The introduced striped bass was brought into the state in 1958 with early releases being made in Herrington and Kentucky Lakes and in Lake Cumberland. They have since been introduced to Dewey Lake and to Green River Reservoir.

The state record striped bass, weighing 44 pounds, 4 ounces, was caught in Herrington Lake on July 19, 1970. Two white bass are tied for the Kentucky record at an even 5 pounds. One was caught in Kentucky Lake on July 11, 1943, and the other in Herrington Lake on July 5, 1957. A record for the yellow bass has not been established.

The outlook for all three basses is excellent. Striped bass are reared from fry to 3—4-inch fingerlings. Both the white and striped bass feed on threadfin or gizzard shad which are abundant in Kentucky waters.

Spring and fall are considered superior bass fishing seasons, though there are no closed fishing seasons in Kentucky.

Commonwealth of Kentucky
Department of Fish and Wildlife Resources
State Office Building Annex
Frankfort, Kentucky 40601

Louisiana

The striped bass, white bass and yellow bass all fin Louisiana waters. The white and yellow bass are both native, and the striped bass was introduced to lakes in the state in 1965.

All three of the basses are highly regarded game fish. The striped bass has just recently become a much sought-after game fish, with D'Arbonne Lake a favorite spot for those who fish for stripers.

Records have not been maintained on striped and yellow bass, but the state record for white bass is 3 pounds, 14 ounces. This fish was caught in 1969.

Lake Bistineau near Minden, Black Lake at Campti, and Lake Bruin at Ferriday are considered good yellow bass waters. White bass are caught in the river lakes and in some of the bayous. Those near Jonesville have good white bass fishing as does Bayou D'Arbonne near Monroe. D'Arbonne Lake near Farmerville is the best striped bass lake at the present, but Toledo Bend Reservoir on the Louisiana-Texas border shows promise.

There are no closed fishing seasons in Louisiana, but spring is considered the best time to fish for these species. On Black Lake the yellow bass fishing is good from the end of February through March and again in June.

All three of the basses are considered game fish with creel limits of 2 stripers, 25 white bass and 50 yellow bass per day. The limit on yellow bass is combined with crappie; in other words, the angler may not take over 50 crappie and yellow bass combined.

Most of the state's management effort at the present is directed toward the striped bass, though the future for all three species looks promising.

> State of Louisiana
> Wild Life and Fisheries Building
> 400 Royal Street
> New Orleans, Louisiana 70130

Maine

In Maine, the white perch is found in all major river drainages, in ponds that were once accessible from the sea, and in naturally inaccessible lakes where it has been introduced by man. When found in the same waters with salmon or trout, the white perch is a serious competitor. Perch, as they are commonly called in Maine, are the most popular panfish in the state, and furnish top sport on light tackle.

The fish thrive in a variety of surroundings, ranging from brackish water to some of the best cold-water lakes.

The white perch is considered a very clean fish and is popular throughout the state. The future of the species is considered excellent, though overpopulation is a problem.

Fishing is generally best in the spring, but is fair in all seasons. The usual season for open-water fishing begins April 1st and runs into September. Ice fishing is generally legal from ice-in until March.

The striped bass is found all along the rocky coast of Maine and fishing for the big stripers is popular in such resort areas as Bar Harbor and Mount Desert Island.

A 4-pound, 12-ounce white perch taken from Messalonskee Lake on June 4, 1949, by Mrs. Earl Small, set a new world record. The big perch was 19½ inches long.

> State of Maine
> Department of Inland Fisheries
>   and Game
> State House
> Augusta, Maine 04330

Maryland

Both the striped bass and white perch are familiar fish in the Chesapeake Bay region of this state. The striped bass is considered the No. 1 game fish in Maryland and is an extremely popular fish. The white perch, popular though it is, is a problem fish in the Chesapeake Bay because of its abundance, small size and slow rate of growth. Management of the perch consists primarily of monitoring the commercial catches.

A good deal of management effort is directed toward the striped bass. However, regulations are for the most part limited to the establishment and enforcement of maximum- and minimum-size limits during certain periods of the year. Usually a minimum size of 12 inches and a maximum size of 15 pounds applies from early March through May. Otherwise the angler is allowed one fish in excess of 15 pounds daily. The 12-inch minimum applies all year. The minimum-size limit also applies in fresh water, though there is no maximum-size limit.

(Left) A youthful Maryland angler admires a big striper taken from the Upper Chesapeake Bay. (Right) A lucky New Mexico angler unhooks a nice white bass. Photo courtesy of New Mexico Department of Game and Fish.

There are uncomfirmed reports of yellow bass in western Maryland.

The state record striped bass of 50 pounds, 1 ounce, was established July 22, 1965, and the record white perch, a 2-pound, 8-ouncer, was caught November 26, 1967.

The activities of commercial fishermen and pollution are the two major clouds on the horizon for these two fish, both of which mean so much to the state.

Don Carpenter, outdoor writer from Annapolis, likes the fall and winter for white perch, though many are taken all year, and particularly during the spring. For stripers, Don recommends June, September, October and November.

> State of Maryland
> Fish and Wildlife Administration
> State Office Building
> Annapolis, Maryland 21401

Massachusetts

Populations of white perch are abundant in both fresh- and saltwater environments in Massachusetts. Overpopulation of white perch is a real problem in many lakes and ponds. For example, when Lake Chauncey was reclaimed, over half of the fish killed in the 185-acre lake were white perch. Many of the freshwater ponds on Cape Cod hold good white perch.

Where the fish grow to respectable sizes they are highly desirable game fish, and are considered tops for table use.

Many perch anglers use grass shrimp and fish the inlets or outlets of ponds in May and June.

The striped bass is a long-standing favorite of the saltwater anglers in Massachusetts, particularly among the hardy ones who fish the rolling surf off of Cape Cod. June and September are favorite months for striped bass fishing in Massachusetts waters. A 72-pound striper taken at Cuttyhunk, Massachusetts, on October 10, 1969, by Edwin J. Kirker set a new saltwater record. The bass measured 54½ inches in length.

> Commonwealth of Massachusetts
> Division of Fisheries and Game
> Leverett Saltonstall Building,
>   100 Cambridge Street
> Government Center
> Boston, Massachusetts 02202

Michigan

The only bass found in Michigan is the white bass. A number of years ago these fish were very abundant in the Great Lakes and connecting waters, but white bass runs in Michigan are now very limited. Apparently the alewives and sea lampreys that upset the balance of the Great Lakes did considerable damage to the bass.

Several years ago the Department of Natural Resources borrowed some striped bass eggs from the South Carolina Fisheries Department and hatched them very successfully. However, nothing came of the project and there are now no plans to introduce other basses to the state.

> State of Michigan
> Department of Natural Resources
> Stevens T. Mason Building
> Lansing, Michigan 48926

Minnesota

Both the white bass and the yellow bass are native to Minnesota, but the yellow bass is very rare.

While both fish are capable of providing good sport, anglers do not regard them highly. This attitude could well change as many conditions in the waters of the state favor the white bass over other now more popular game fish.

The yellow bass is found only in a few lakes in the south central part of the state. The white bass is very abundant in the lower St. Croix River and in the Mississippi River below its confluence with the St. Croix. It is also very abundant in Big Stone Lake.

The best fishing months are the spring and early summer months.

While the future of white bass fishing looks promising, there are at present no management plans for the fish.

> State of Minnesota
> Department of Conservation
> 658 Cedar Street
> St. Paul, Minnesota 55101

Mississippi

All of the true basses except the white perch are found in Mississippi waters. All of these fish are native to the state, but the striped bass is being introduced to inland reservoirs just as it has been introduced to such waters in many other states. The striper is native to the salt and brackish waters of Mississippi, though the fishing is not as good as it is in the Atlantic Coast states.

Top striper waters include the Ross Barnett Reservoir and Pascagoula River. The white bass is abundant in Eagle Lake and Grenada Reservoir, and Eagle Lake is also considered a good yellow bass lake.

All of the basses except the little yellow bass are considered excellent game species, and the future appears rosy for these fish. While fishing is legal all year, spring and fall are considered the best bass seasons.

> State of Mississippi
> Game and Fish Building
> Box 451
> 402 High Street
> Jackson, Mississippi 39205

Missouri

The striped bass, white bass and yellow bass are all found in the waters of the "Show-Me State." White and yellow basses are native; the striper was introduced.

The striped bass was introduced to the Lake of the Ozarks. The yellow bass is primarily a fish of the Mississippi River and is reasonably abundant in the navigation pools of the river above St. Louis. The white bass is found in all of the larger reservoirs in the state, but was introduced to many of them. In others it was native to the rivers which feed the impoundments.

Both the white and yellow bass are considered good game fish, though fishing for the yellow bass is more limited. The striped bass populations have not expanded to the point where they provide good fishing.

Three white bass are tied for the state record of 4 pounds, 8 ounces. One was taken from Norfolk Reservoir in 1952, and the others were caught in Bull Shoals Reservoir since then.

The future of white bass fishing is particularly good, and the striper potential is promising. The best white bass fishing occurs in the early spring as the fish make their spawning runs up tributary streams of the reservoirs. The next best fishing comes in the summer as the fish chase shad schools near the surface. Fishing is legal all year with liberal white bass limits of 15 daily.

> State of Missouri
> Missouri Department of Conservation
> Fish and Game Research Center
> 1110 College Avenue
> Columbia, Missouri 65201

Montana

This is one of the few states that have no true basses. At present there are no plans to introduce them in Montana.

> State of Montana
> Department of Fish and Game
> Helena, Montana 59601

Nebraska

Nebraska has populations of both the striped and white bass. The white perch has also been introduced to the state, the farthest westward penetration by this little native of the Atlantic drainage system. The white bass is a native, but the striped bass and white perch are introduced species.

The white bass is by far the most abundant and is very popular as a game fish. The fish were first discovered in the state in 1892, but the populations declined until by the early 1940's white bass was very rare. In 1944 the fish were stocked in Lake McConaughy and they are now abundant there and in other reservoirs around the state. The best fishing waters are Lake McConaughy, Harlan County Reservoir and Gavins Point.

The striped bass was introduced to Lake McConaughy in 1961, and several heavy stockings have been made since. This lake is just beginning to offer good striper fishing. The daily limit on striped bass is 2.

Lake McConaughy claims the record for striped bass, a 10-pound, 1-ounce fish caught September 29, 1970. The record white bass, a 4-pound, 15-ounce lunker, was taken from a sandpit near Grand Island in 1962.

June, July, September and October have proven to be the best months for striper fishing. Spring is the best season for white bass.

The white perch is established in Walgren Lake and also in a smaller lake near Lincoln.

It appears that both the white bass and striper have good futures as reservoir fish in Nebraska. The future of the white perch is undecided; it will no doubt be determined by angler interest.

State of Nebraska
Game and Parks Commission
State House
Lincoln, Nebraska 68509

Nevada

None of the basses are native to Nevada, but white bass have been introduced to Lahontan Reservoir and striped bass to the Colorado River. Fishing for the respective species is best in these two bodies of water. White bass have also been introduced to Rye Patch Reservoir where they have apparently reproduced. Striped bass are being stocked in Lake Mead.

A 3-pound, 1-ounce white bass holds the present state record, and a 24-pound striper is the current striped bass champion. Both were caught in 1969.

Seasons on both fish are open all year, but the best white bass fishing occurs from June through September. The striper fishing is also best during the summer months—June through August.

The basses are being studied and closely observed by the Department of Fish and Game with the possibility of their being expanded to other waters.

State of Nevada
Department of Fish and Game
P.O. Box 10678
Reno, Nevada 89510

New Hampshire

The coastal waters of New Hampshire have migrant populations of striped bass and resident populations of white perch. The white perch is also landlocked in many inland waters.

The Great Bay estuary is considered one of the finest striped bass fishing grounds on the northeast coast. The Hampton Bay area is also good. Winnisquam Lake in Laconia, Kanasatke Lake in Moultonboro, and Webster Lake in Franklin are popular waters for the white perch.

Unfortunately, the little bass become overpopulated in many inland waters.

While both white perch and striped bass are indigenous to the state, white perch have been introduced to new waters. The striper is a very popular fish, and while the white perch does not receive a good deal of attention during the open-water season, it is popular among ice-fishermen.

The Fish and Game Department does not keep official records, but an 18-inch, 3-pound white perch taken in 1965 is indicative of the quality of the perch fishing. Stripers in excess of 50 pounds are taken every season.

There are no closed seasons or creel limits on either fish, but striper fishing excels from June through September. White perch are caught all year.

Management of the species is limited to control of overpopulation of white perch and the improvement of forage fish for the striped bass. Fishing for both bass should continue strong.

> State of New Hampshire
> Fish and Game Department
> 34 Bridge Street
> Concord, New Hampshire 03301

New Jersey

White perch and striped bass are native to New Jersey and are found in all tidal rivers and bays except those where pollution has eliminated them. Striped bass are also found in the surf, usually within two or three miles of the beach, but occasionally as far as ten to twelve miles offshore.

April, May and November are considered choice months for striper fishing. Sandy Hook is usually good in April and November, Barnegat and Great Bays in April and May, and the Delaware River and Bay in April and November.

White perch fishing is best from November through January. Good perch waters include Great Egg, Maurice, Mullica and Tuckahoe Rivers and Collins Cove.

White perch have been stocked exclusively in ponds throughout New Jersey and striped bass have been stocked in some waters. Good ones are Union Lake in Cumberland County and Farrington Lake in Middlesex County.

Striped bass are considered top game fish in New Jersey, and anglers hold them in high esteem. White perch, generally considered as panfish, are not as widely sought after. As elsewhere they tend to become stunted in ponds.

The saltwater record for striped bass is 64 pounds, 8 ounces. The big fish was taken from Great Egg Harbor River in 1968. The freshwater record, a 23-pound, 8-ouncer, was taken from Union Lake in 1952. A lady angler, Mrs. Albert Beebe, was the lucky fisherwoman. There are no saltwater records for perch, but a 2-pound, 8-ounce fish caught in Lake Hopatcong in 1950, holds the freshwater record.

Management of the true basses is limited to netting restrictions on both fish, and closed seasons and size limits for stripers.

> State of New Jersey
> Department of Conservation and
>   Economic Development
> Division of Fish and Game
> P.O. Box 1809
> Trenton, New Jersey 08625

New Mexico

The white bass is the sole representative of the true bass family in New Mexico. However, the fish is well regarded by anglers of the state and apparently has a good future in this southwestern state. Good waters include the Pecos River above Red Bluff Reservoir and the same river between McMillan and Avalon Reservoirs. Also good is the Rio Grande River between Elephant Butte and Caballo Reservoirs. Good reservoirs include Elephant Butte and Caballo.

The fish were introduced to these waters. The white bass is not a native of the state. A fine 4-pound specimen holds the state record.

Fishing for white bass is legal year-around, but the best fishing comes in the spring during the spawning runs and in the fall near the headwaters of the big reservoirs. The daily limit on this popular fish is a liberal 40.

> State of New Mexico
> Department of Game and Fish
> State Capitol
> Santa Fe, New Mexico 87501

New York

Three of the true basses, the white perch, the white bass, and the striped bass are found in the state of New York. They are all native to the waters of the state.

Good striped bass fishing is found in the lower Hudson River and in the coastal waters of Long Island. White bass fishing is good in Lake Ontario and Oneida Lake, and good white perch waters include the lower Hudson River, Lake Ontario, Oneida Lake, and scattered small lakes near the Hudson River. All of the fish are highly regarded by New York anglers.

White perch are becoming more widespread in the state, and the future looks good for this little bass. It is also felt that pollution abatement in the Hudson River will create a bright future for the already popular striper. The outlook for white bass is less predictable.

Thousands of surf anglers fish the coastal waters of Long Island, particularly along Jones Inlet and Fire Island Inlet areas on the South Shore. Surf-fishermen favor natural baits for the spring striper fishing, but switch to artificial lures in the fall. These are the peak angling periods. It is generally accepted that night fishermen fare better than those who work the surf during the daylight hours.

Trollers ply the striped bass waters in the vicinity of Moutauk Point with considerable success.

White bass fishing in New York is generally good from late spring through summer, and the white perch provide good fishing from late spring through the fall months. Fall is considered the peak season for striped bass, though they are found in the Hudson River all spring and summer.

Fishery managers encourage New York anglers to utilize the white perch and white bass as fully as possible. A minimum-size limit of 16 inches has been placed on the striped bass, but anglers are encouraged to take fish in excess of that.

State of New York
Department of Environmental Conservation
Albany, New York 12201

North Carolina

The "Tarheel State" is within the range of both the white perch and striped bass and these fish are native to the state. The white bass has been introduced and is proving to be an exciting reservoir fish.

White perch and striped bass provide good fishing in the Albemarle Sound areas. Lake Waccamaw, a shallow inland lake, is a favorite fishing spot for white perch. This is a large, shallow body of water between Whitville and Wilmington. Successful anglers fish the lake by trolling— until they hit a school, at least.

During fall and winter, striper fishing is good in the Atlantic surf from the Virginia line to Cape Hatteras. Manns Harbor in Croatan Sound and nearby East Lake are also good winter waters. Spawning runs up the Dan and Roanoke Rivers provide exciting spring striper fishing. Fishing for landlocked stripers is good in Kerr Reservoir and Lake Gaston (both on the Virginia border) and at times, in Lake Norman.

Good white bass lakes include Lakes Tillery and Wylie and Fontana Reservoir.

Management of the basses is generally limited to the introduction of the white and striped basses to suitable inland reservoirs and some research in coastal waters. W. Donald Baker, Supervisor of Fisheries for the Division of Inland Fisheries, says they raise striped bass in hatcheries and release them into suitable waters when they are about two inches long. Baker calls this the "put-grow-and-take" method.

Interest in the true basses runs high in North Carolina, particularly with respect to the striped bass. The striper is a popular winter fish. The future of these bass is extremely bright in North Carolina.

State of North Carolina
Wildlife Resources Commission
Raleigh, North Carolina 27602

A pair of white bass taken from North Carolina's Fontana Reservoir.

North Dakota

Of the four members of the true bass family, only the white bass is found in North Dakota. The white bass was introduced to North Dakota waters in 1953.

North Dakota anglers are very fond of white bass and spend many happy hours fishing for them. A 4-pound, 4-ounce fish taken in 1969 holds the state record.

Best fishing waters include the Missouri River and Lakes Ashtabula, Sakakawea, and Tschida.

The future of white bass fishing looks excellent. There are no closed seasons but May, June and July are considered the best months.

State of North Dakota
Division of Fisheries
North Dakota Game
    and Fish Department
Bismarck, North Dakota 58501

Ohio

The white bass is native to Ohio and is found in many varied waters of the state. The striped bass was first introduced to the state in 1967 and the Ohio Department of Natural Resources is still experimenting with this member of the bass family. Indications are that it can provide some interesting fishing for Ohio anglers, but as yet there is no open season on the striper.

(Left) An Ohio angler with a good catch of white bass. Photo courtesy of Ohio Division of Wildlife. (Right) A happy angler admires a fine South Carolina striper.

The Bass and Kelleys Islands area of Lake Erie probably offers as good white bass fishing as can be found anywhere. The fishing is also good at Mouse Island, the Mouth of Sandusky Bay and Port Clinton-Reef areas. Spring and summer months are peak seasons. Other good waters include the Huron, Maumee and Sandusky Rivers and Pleasant Hill Reservoir; also Berlin, Mosquito Creek, Seneca and Pymatuning Reservoirs.

The record white bass, a 3-pound, 6-ouncer, measured 18 inches in length and was caught in the Kelleys Island section of Lake Erie on August 24, 1954.

The future of white bass fishing in Ohio seems almost unlimited.

There are no closed seasons on white bass, but the best fishing occurs from June to September in Lake Erie and in May and June on inland waters.

> State of Ohio
> Ohio Department of Natural Resources
> Division of Wildlife
> 1500 Dublin Road
> Columbus, Ohio 43215

Oklahoma

Of the four members of the true bass family, only the white perch is not found in Oklahoma waters. The white bass is the most abundant, though striped bass are beginning to reproduce in Keystone Reservoir. The yellow bass is limited to a few small lakes in southeastern Oklahoma.

White and yellow bass are natives of the state, but the striped bass was introduced—apparently successfully.

While the white bass is not classed as a game fish, the majority of Oklahoma anglers consider it a sporting fish, and fish for it rather enthusiastically. They are found in most of the large reservoirs in the state, but 93,000-acre Lake Texoma is considered the best white bass lake in Oklahoma.

The striped bass is considered one of the most valuable game fish in the state, and anglers and fishery managers have high hopes for this big bass. At present, Keystone Reservoir is the top striper lake; however, the Oklahoma record of 15 pounds was taken in the river below the Keystone Dam on December 14, 1970. This record could be broken at any time as striper populations begin to mature.

The record white bass, a 4-pound whopper, was taken from Fort Supply Reservoir on May 31, 1966.

The future of both the white and striped bass seems assured; however, the big stripers seem to generate the most enthusiasm at this writing. Biologists feel they will establish biological control in many of the state's big reservoirs where gizzard shad tend to overpopulate.

Winter fishing is very good in Lake Texoma where anglers fish the bottom for white bass, but in the summer the bass tend to surface and feed on threadfin shad. "Jump" fishing is popular. In other reservoirs, bass surface in the spring and feed on gizzard shad which are more prevalent in Oklahoma than the threadfin in Texoma. White bass fishing is probably best in the spring when the fish make their spawning runs up tributary rivers of the reservoirs.

The best striped bass fishing also comes in the spring—in the tail waters of Keystone Dam.

Fishing for both white and yellow bass is legal all year, but there is a closed season from April 15 through May 31 in Lake Texoma.

The basic management for both white and striped bass consists of providing stock for suitable waters—primarily the big reservoirs.

State of Oklahoma
Department of Wildlife Conservation
Oklahoma Fishery Research Laboratory
1416 Planck Street
Norman, Oklahoma 73069

Oregon

The striped bass, which was introduced to California in 1879 and eventually worked its way up the Pacific Coast, is the only member of the bass family found in Oregon. A few fish are taken as far north as the mouth of the Columbia River, but these are considered strays. Its general range is the southern half of the Oregon coast.

The fish is very abundant in Winchester and Coos Bay, where extensive tidal areas permit the fish to run and spawn. Smaller populations of stripers appear in Siuslaw, Coquille and Rogue Rivers.

The striper is very popular among a large segment of Oregon anglers. Most fishing takes place in the tidal sections of the Umpqua and Smith Rivers, Winchester Bay, the Millicoma River and Coos River and Bay.

Surprisingly surf-fishing is not popular in Oregon although the fish feed all along the south coast.

Angling is open all year, but most fishing is done in the spring and summer. It slows down considerably in the fall and practically ceases during the winter months.

River pollution is the only major cloud on the horizon for these fine West Coast striped bass.

State of Oregon
Fishery Commission
Office of the Director
P.O. Box 3503
1634 SW Alder Street
Portland, Oregon 97208

Pennsylvania

While the white perch, white bass and striped bass are all native to Pennsylvania, there is very little angling interest in these fish. However, the Pennsylvania Fish Commission is starting to experiment with striped bass in inland waters. This may eventually generate new interest in these fine fish.

At present the only striped bass fishery in the state is in the lower stretch of the Delaware River. The open season for these fish is March 1 to December 31, and the minimum-size limit is 12 inches. There is no creel limit. Heavy industrial pollution in the Delaware River limits the potential of striped bass fishing in the river.

Through the exchange of muskellunge fry for striped bass eggs from North Carolina, fingerling stripers have been reared in Pennsylvania hatcheries and released in Shenango Reservoir near Sharpsville and in Middle Creek Dam near Selinsgrove. This is the northernmost attempt to introduce striped bass to inland waters.

Commonwealth of Pennsylvania
Pennsylvania Fish Commission
P.O. Box 1673
Harrisburg, Pennsylvania 17120

Rhode Island

White perch and striped bass are native to the waters of Rhode Island. Both are very popular fish among the anglers of this small state on the New England Coast.

The waters of Block Island Sound and Narragansett Bay are prime striped bass waters and fished heavily by striper anglers from all over New England. White perch are found in all of the small estuaries and in many freshwater lakes and ponds.

While both the bass and perch are native to Rhode Island, the white perch has been widely stocked in inland waters and is now present in at least a third of the inland lakes and ponds.

Anglers favor both fish and the outlook for the future of perch and striper fishing is excellent. Fishing is permitted all year.

The striped bass fishing is generally best in the summer and fall, but spring is the favored season for brackish water white perch fishing. Perch fishing is good year-around in the freshwater ponds and lakes.

A 67-pound striped bass holds the Rhode Island record and it was caught in the mid-1960's. There are no official perch records, but fishery biologists estimate fish in the vicinity of 3–4 pounds are taken from the brackish waters of the state. The minimum-size limit on striped bass is 16 inches, otherwise there is little management of the true basses in Rhode Island. Little is needed at this time.

State of Rhode Island
Rhode Island Department
    of Natural Resources
Veterans Memorial Building
Providence, Rhode Island 02903

South Carolina

The landlocked striped bass is the big news in South Carolina. In fact, the handsome fish has made the big Santee-Cooper Reservoirs famous throughout the 50 states and in a few foreign countries. It was here that biologists established the fact that the anadromous fish could spawn, live and die in fresh water, never returning to the briny waters as it had done since the origin of the species.

The white bass is also present in South Carolina waters, though it was introduced. An interesting hybrid, the white bass/striped bass, has been produced by fishery biologists and is doing well.

The best waters for striped bass are the impounded ones of the Santee-Cooper lakes complex—Marion and Moultrie Reservoirs. These lakes were formed by damming the Congaree and Wateree Rivers, good striped bass waters in their own right, and productive of the fish long before the reservoirs were built.

The white bass is found in all of the major reservoirs in the state, but the hybrid is limited to Hartwell and Clark Hill Reservoirs.

All of the basses are highly regarded game fish, prized by local anglers. The landlocked striper is well established and its future seems assured. Fishery biologists view the future of the white bass and hybrid with cautious optimism.

The state record striped bass, weighing 55 pounds, was caught in Lake Moultrie in January of 1963. The record hybrid weighed 5 pounds, 14 ounces and was caught in Clark Hill Reservoir. It measured 21 inches in length.

There are no closed seasons on the true basses and the fish are caught all year. However, spring and autumn are the best seasons. Anglers take advantage of the fish's spawning activities in the spring and its schooling habits in the fall.

Both the striped bass and hybrids are produced in South Carolina hatcheries. Experimental stockings are being made throughout the state.

> State of South Carolina
> South Carolina Wildlife
>   Resources Department
> Post Office Box 167
> Columbia, South Carolina 29202

South Dakota

The white bass is the only member of the true bass family found in South Dakota. It is a native of the state.

The white bass is fairly abundant in the Missouri River impoundments and in the natural lakes of eastern South Dakota. At the best it is regarded as a marginal fish by South Dakota anglers.

The record white bass was a good one. It weighed 4 pounds, 3 ounces, and was taken from Enemy Swim Lake by Todd D. Lohman in 1970.

White bass tend to be cyclic with the fish extremely abundant at the peak of the cycle.

Except for the northeast counties where the season is closed in March and April, year-around fishing is permitted. The spring and summer months normally provide the best fishing.

At present, management of the basses is limited to the introduction of the fish to new waters.

> State of South Dakota
> South Dakota Department
>   of Game, Fish and Parks
> State Office Building
> Pierre, South Dakota 57501

Tennessee

All of the true basses except white perch are found in "The Volunteer State"—plus an exciting new addition to the family, the hybrid. White and yellow bass are native to the state, but the striped bass was introduced. The hybrid of the white and striped basses was produced by Tennessee biologists in cooperation with South Carolina biologists. This joint effort was started in 1965.

Both the white bass and striped bass are found generally throughout Tennessee, and the yellow bass is common in the western part of the state.

Most of the impoundments on the Cumberland and Tennessee Rivers provide good white bass fishing. Some of the best white bass waters include Cherokee, Holston and Norris Lakes and the Clinch and French Broad Rivers in east Tennessee. Barkley, Kentucky and Reelfoot Lakes offer good yellow bass fishing.

The striped bass is just becoming reasonably abundant, and at present the best fishing is found in Cherokee and Percy Priest Lakes. Norris and Old Hickory Lakes also have some striper fishing.

Cherokee Lake provides most of the hybrid fishing, but Norris and Patrick Henry Lakes have limited hybrid fishing.

Tennessee anglers consider the striped bass and hybrid the top members of the bass family, but thousands of anglers fish the Holston and Clinch Rivers each spring to catch spawning white bass.

The record striped bass taken March 3, 1970, weighed 20 pounds, 9 ounces, and the record white bass (taken in 1949) tipped the scales at 4 pounds, 10 ounces. Tennessee claims the world record hybrid, a big 14-pound, 12-ounce specimen caught November 14, 1970.

The future of all four fish in Tennessee appears bright. The striped bass and hybrid are growing in importance each year. Stripers were practically nonexistent in 1963, but by 1970 anglers were taking 25,000 annually. The average weight then was 7 pounds.

The best fishing for Tennessee basses comes in the spring when the fish migrate up the rivers on their annual spawning runs. Fall fishing is also good.

Very little management effort is directed toward the white and yellow basses which seem to do quite well on their own. Both the striped bass and the hybrid are raised in state hatcheries and released in selected reservoirs.

State of Tennessee
Tennessee Game and Fish Commission
Ellington Agriculture Center
P.O. Box 9400
Nashville, Tennessee 37220

Texas

Both the yellow and white bass are native to the "Lone Star State," and striped bass have been introduced to several major reservoirs. The white bass is the most common and the most popular. It occurs state-wide. The little yellow bass is found in most of the waters of eastern Texas. The striper has been widely introduced.

Select striped bass waters include Lake Texoma, Lake Bardwell, Navarro Mills Reservoir and Toledo Bend. White bass are also popular in Lake Texoma, but other good waters include Lake Texarkana, and the Colorado River and lakes. Yellow bass are found in Tawakoni, White Rock and Caddo Lakes.

Anglers consider the white and striped bass desirable game fish, but they feel the yellow bass is too small.

The state record white bass, caught in the Colorado River in March of 1968, weighed 5 pounds, 4½ ounces. The striper record of 12 pounds, 12 ounces, was established in April of 1969. The striper record is no doubt destined to fall, but the white bass record seems reasonably safe.

Most management effort at the present time is directed toward stocking striped bass in new waters, though a good deal of research and management has been undertaken on the white bass.

Striper fry from South Carolina and Virginia are reared to stocking size in Texas hatcheries.

While there are no closed seasons on the true basses, the best fishing for all can be expected during the spring spawning runs. "Jump" fishing for white bass is popular in the summer months.

State of Texas
Parks and Wildlife Department
John H. Reagan State Office Building
Austin, Texas 78701

Utah

None of the true basses are native to Utah, but white bass have been successfully introduced. Striped bass have also been introduced, but this endeavor is still in the experimental stage.

Utah Lake is considered the best white bass lake in the state. However, others are of minor importance.

Utah anglers like the white bass which hits hard and fights well. The record white bass, a 4-pound, 1-ouncer, was taken in 1970.

The white bass is considered a favorite sport fish in Utah and the future of white bass fishing is bright. The season is open all year, but the best fishing can be expected in March right after the ice goes out. Bass are found close to shore at that time. While the spring fishing is best, even summer fishing is fair. Winter fishing is good near warm springs in Utah Lake.

Management of the species is limited to the introduction of fry to new waters, and the prevention of pollution of present bass waters.

> State of Utah
> Utah Department of Natural Resources
> Division of Fish and Game
> 1596 West North Temple
> Salt Lake City, Utah 84116

Vermont

The white perch is the only member of the true bass family found in Vermont. While remnant native populations may exist in Marshfield Dam, the major populations at the present time are the result of introductions to several lakes.

The white perch is not considered a game fish at this time and there are no plans to expand its populations.

There are no closed seasons on white perch in Vermont.

> State of Vermont
> Fish and Game Department
> Montpelier, Vermont 05602

Virginia

With both striped bass and white perch abundant throughout her rich tidal waters, and the landlocked striped bass and white bass finning a number of inland reservoirs, the "Old Dominion" has a good variety of true bass fishing.

Fishing for striped bass is good throughout the Chesapeake Bay area and along the Virginia beaches in the spring. The major tidal rivers (the James, Rappahannock, Potomac) and others also offer good striped bass fishing. The landlocked stripers are most abundant in Buggs Island Reservoir where they were established a few years after the discovery of the Santee-Cooper striper fishery in South Carolina. The spring spawning runs up the Dan and Roanoke Rivers provide exciting fishing. Other good waters include Gaston Reservoir and Smith Mountain Lake.

The best white bass fishing is found in Claytor Lake, the New River and Occoquan Reservoir.

White perch fishing is good in the entire eastern part of the state, to and just above the tide line. Good waters include the Potomac River and Back Bay.

All of the fish are native to the state, but both the striper and white bass have also been stocked widely in promising waters.

(Top) Virginia's Chesapeake Bay Bridge-Tunnel is a hot spot for winter stripers.
(Bottom) Bank fishermen dunk minnows to Tennessee white bass.

The striped bass is a favorite of many Virginia anglers, particularly those who fish the Chesapeake Bay. The striper spawning run out of Buggs Island Lake also draws anglers from long distances. The white bass is gaining in popularity and the little white perch is an old favorite.

State records include a 32-pound, 3-ounce striper taken from Gaston Lake on May 23, 1969, a 3-pound, 3-ounce white bass caught in Occoquan Reservoir in September of 1970 and a 2-pound white perch caught in Back Bay in 1969. The record saltwater striped bass weighed 58 pounds, 8 ounces.

The future of all the basses in Virginia seems assured at the moment. Jack Hoffman, Chief of the Fish Division of the Commission of Game and Inland Fisheries, says the true basses are relatively pollution-tolerant and a concerted effort is being made to clean up the state's rivers.

The most popular season to fish for landlocked stripers is the spring as the fish make their spawning runs up the Dan and Roanoke Rivers. The spring months are also tops for white bass and white perch. However, the seasons are continuous for these fish and some are probably caught every month of the year. Late fall and early winter are popular seasons for working the Chesapeake Bay for stripers.

Size limits for stripers are 14 inches for the saltwater fish and 12 inches for the landlocked bass. It is illegal for commercial fishermen to sell striped bass that are 40 inches or more in length or 25 pounds or greater in weight.

All three fish have been successfully propagated by fishery biologists, however white perch and white bass are very successful natural spawners. Most management effort at the present is being directed toward the hatchery production of striped bass and their release in suitable waters. White bass are also stocked from time to time.

The Commonwealth of Virginia
Commission of Game
and Inland Fisheries
Box 11104
Richmond, Virginia 23230
and
Claude Rogers, Director
Virginia Salt Water Fishing Tournament
25th Street and Pacific Avenue
Virginia Beach, Virginia 23451

Washington

Except for an occasional stray striped bass along the coast, there are no true basses in Washington.

State of Washington
Department of Game
600 North Capitol Way
Olympia, Washington 98501

West Virginia

The white bass is native to West Virginia waters, and the striped bass has been introduced.

The best white bass fishing is found in Bluestone Reservoir and its tail waters. Good white bass fishing can be found throughout the New River at certain times of the year, however. There is some striped bass fishing in the Ohio River where striped bass were introduced in 1967.

The white bass is a very popular fish in those waters where it is fairly abundant. The future of the white bass seems assured as the fishing improves from year to year. The state record of 4 pounds was taken from the Kanawha River in 1964.

The future of the striper is unpredictable at this time.

In Bluestone Reservoir the best fishing can be expected in May and June, but the best catches from the Little Kanawha River come in June and July. However, there are no closed seasons on white bass and striped bass in West Virginia.

Management efforts at the present time are limited to the striped bass. In recent years over 45,000 fingerlings have been raised in the Palestine Hatchery and released in the Ohio River. Biologists feel the abundant populations of gizzard shad in the Ohio River bid well for striped bass in these waters.

> State of West Virginia
> Department of Natural Resources
> Route 2
> Belleville, West Virginia 26133

Wisconsin

Both the white and yellow bass are native to Wisconsin, but anglers show little interest in them at the present time. Good waters include the Wisconsin River, Wolf River, Lake Winnebago, Lake Mendota, Lake Monona and other southern Wisconsin waters.

Fishing for the basses is legal all year, but the best time to catch them is during the May spawning run.

> State of Wisconsin
> Department of Natural Resources
> Box 450
> Madison, Wisconsin 53701

Wyoming

There are no members of the true bass family in Wyoming waters, and at present there are no plans to stock them.

> State of Wyoming
> Game and Fish Commission
> Cheyenne, Wyoming 82001

Chapter 4

HABITAT

The true basses are big-water fish. The ocean, large bays, big lakes, and even big rivers are their domain. Even the white perch, the smallest of the quartet, prefers big waters, and is rarely found in small streams, even during its spring spawning runs. Attempts to introduce striped and white bass to new waters have been most successful in the big reservoirs, those providing thousands of acres of open water.

The true basses also tend to be open-water fish, traveling in schools and covering lots of territory. Undercut banks, crevices in rocks and boulders, and other such cover so often sought by the more popular game fish, hold little appeal for this interesting family of fish.

The big striped bass, the largest of the true basses, and probably the most popular, is by nature a fish of the sea. However, the striper is seldom found far from shore, a characteristic which makes it a favorite of the surf-fisherman and small-boat angler. Rocky shores, reefs, bars, and the surf along the beaches are all favorite hangouts for the striped bass, and these are the waters in which veteran anglers seek this handsome bass of the salt and brackish waters. Inlets between the ocean and bays or sounds are also good bass fishing points.

The striper's love for rocks and rocky shorelines has led many anglers to give it the common name of rock or rockfish.

Throughout most of its range the striped bass moves into the rivers and bays for spawning in the spring and it may migrate many miles upstream. However, in the dead of winter it seeks the very deep water and usually remains there until the weather moderates.

Another characteristic which endears the striper to the hearts of the anglers is its preference for shallow water. It spends much of the year in such water, making itself available for surf-casters and trollers working from small boats.

Jetties are popular fishing spots along the New Jersey coast. Bridge abutments are always a likely spot for stripers. One of the most popular fishing areas in the Chesapeake Bay is the Bay-Bridge Tunnel that spans the mouth of the big bay. Most major tidal rivers are spanned by a bridge or two and they offer unusual angling opportunities. Many fish are also taken near causeways along the Atlantic Coast.

The shallow, grassy water in the bays and coves provides interesting fishing and this is the type of water favored by anglers who like to fish for stripers with big saltwater fly rods or bait-casting tackle.

(Top) Working the grass flats around Virginia's Gwynn River for striped bass.
(Bottom) Wading anglers work a reservoir tributary for the April run of white bass.

(Top) Striped bass frequent the surf of both the Atlantic and Pacific Oceans.
(Bottom) Striped bass and bluefish often live in the same water in big inland bays
and sounds.

J. Harry Cornell, of the North Carolina Wildlife Resources Commission, says striped bass are not often taken from streams with less than 1,000 square feet cross-sectional areas.

What has been said so far regarding the striped bass has been in light of conditions along the Atlantic Coast. Generally, the same principles apply to the Pacific Coast striper fishery. Much of the western striped bass fishing is concentrated in the San Pablo and San Francisco Bay and Delta area where there is a wide variety of good fishing water.

(Top) The large southern reservoirs hold both white and striped bass. (Bottom) Offshore structures attract striped bass.

The striped bass is a brackish water fish—or anadromous, at home in either fresh or salt water. During the spawning season the striper is found mostly in fresh or brackish water, but it spends the winter in salt water.

The striped bass' tolerance for either fresh or salt water is the basis for a fast growing and exciting new fishery in the big multipurpose reservoirs scattered across the southern half of the United States. These huge reservoirs are usually controversial ventures, but not so for anglers who like to fish for the big landlocked striped bass that are beginning to flourish in many of them.

Many of the guidelines striped bass fishermen have used so successfully for years in locating salt and brackish water bass can also be employed to find the landlocked fish. The big fish still school in lakes, and locating the schools is half the game. Electronic fish-finders are a big help and many successful anglers use them. Landlocked stripers

(Left) A nice striped bass from the Dan River, a tributary of Kerr Reservoir on the North Carolina-Virginia border. (Right) Both white perch and yellow bass sometimes work their ways into small streams.

spend most of the year in the main body of the big reservoirs where anglers troll for them or fish with live or cut bait. Rocky points and the mouths of deep coves are likely areas to locate the fish. Much of the year they live in deep water.

However, the most exciting landlocked striper fishing comes in the spring as the fish move up the feeder streams to spawn. This usually occurs in late April or May on the Dan and Staunton Rivers in my native Virginia. The big fish leave Kerr Reservoir at this season and anglers wait for them at favorite spots many miles upstream. When living in the streams the landlocked stripers seek much the same kind of cover most stream fish do. They take advantage of fallen trees and debris and midstream boulders. They watch the current for the food it can bring them. Successful anglers cast to fallen logs, large rocks and boulders, the eddies near the head of quiet water where the swift current pours in, and rocky or debris-laden shorelines.

Another popular place to fish for landlocked stripers is the tail waters below the big dams that impound thousands of acres of water. Some of these fish work upstream and others apparently spill over from the water behind the dam. In any event, they often provide fast and exciting fishing in the turbid tail waters.

The white bass, like the larger striper, is also a big water fish and most are taken from large natural lakes such as Lake Erie, or from many of the big impoundments discussed previously for stripers. They are also found in most of the larger rivers of the Mississippi River drainage system.

Throughout most of the year schools of white bass roam the big lakes and anglers rely upon their feeding activities to locate them. They watch for surface action where the hungry bass tear into schools of baitfish. The ruckus caused by the frantic minnows can be seen from quite a distance. In the Great Lakes and other areas frequented by gulls the angler can often locate bass by watching the actions of the graceful birds. They follow the feeding bass, picking up tidbits of food and dying minnows left by the foraging fish.

Probably the fastest angling action of the year occurs when white bass head up the feeder streams on their own annual spawning runs. When spawning starts in March or April, the fish can be found in the streams themselves and in arms of the lake into which the feeder streams flow. The spawning fish are usually located in fairly shallow water, making for interesting fishing.

When not on their spawning runs, or feeding near the surface, white bass scatter out in deep water and are difficult to locate. A few are taken by anglers trolling off rocky points or fishing deep coves with live minnows.

I find it hard to establish a pattern with respect to the habitat requirements of the white perch. Within their range, the tiniest bass are so abundant and widely scattered that I more or less accept them where I find them—whatever that means!

Before man started monkeying with the North American environment, white perch were probably found in most salt and brackish waters from Nova Scotia to the Carolinas—and they still live in many of them. They were also present in most freshwater ponds and streams accessible to the wandering little fish. However, like the other members of its family, the white perch likes big water and moves around a good deal, traveling in schools. For these reasons I say white perch are mostly where you find them.

The white perch thrives in a variety of water, ranging from salt and brackish waters to deep, cold, Maine lakes where it competes with salmon and trout. The fish are not afraid of deep water and they have been taken in gill nets 100 feet deep.

In the southern part of its range the white perch is found mainly in the estuaries of rivers and bays. However, in the northern reaches of its range it seems to prefer freshwater streams and ponds.

(Left) Bridges and other concrete and rock structures attract striped bass. (Right) Pilings in tidal streams attract both striped bass and white perch.

In freshwater lakes, young perch are often found close to beaches or shoal areas, but large perch do not venture into shallow water to any extent, except during spawning time.

It is in the spring when the perch congregate in huge schools for spawning runs up tributary streams that the fish are the easiest to locate. At such times neither locating the fish or catching them is much of a challenge, but it is fun. One of the best perch-fishing areas I know is the Chain Bridge section of the Potomac River right in the District of Columbia.

From personal experience I have found that perch also like rocky areas such as points and boulders. Such water is always a good place to start fishing—even though the angler may eventually find a good school elsewhere and take his limit in a hurry. Millions of perch are taken every season from bridges, jetties and docks, but whether the fish seek these areas, I do not know. It may be because such places are more accessible to the angler.

Another good spot to fish for white perch during the spring is the inlet to a freshwater pond. Perch frequent these areas, moving to them from the main body of the lake, and often using them for spawning when major feeder streams are not available.

In the winter months, when ice-fishermen are out, the white perch seeks the deeper parts of the lake.

Lake Gaston, in Virginia, is noted for its striped bass fishing.

Regardless of where he fishes, the perch angler should keep in mind that the fish moves around a lot and may be found just about anywhere in a lake or river, bay or sound.

The little yellow bass, the true bass of the Midwest and the Mississippi River and Great Lakes drainage systems, is also a fish of the big water, primarily large lakes and the Mississippi River itself.

In the big river towns of Illinois the yellow bass is a very popular fish in the larger rivers such as the Illinois and Mississippi. In addition to these major waters, yellow bass are found in the backwaters and adjoining bottomland lakes and major tributaries. Other good yellow bass waters include natural lakes in the Midwest, farm ponds, city water-supply lakes and large impoundments. They are rarely native to such waters, having been introduced to them accidentally or by experimental releases.

During the April or early May spawning season, yellow bass move into the shallows where they are found over gravel bars, rocky reefs or underwater brush and in weeds in shallow water.

In the summer the fish move into deeper water and are difficult to locate, though they do travel in schools and once the school is pinpointed, the angler can anticipate good fishing.

Where big impoundments are located in good yellow bass water, the fishing can be successful below the dam in the tailraces.

In Louisiana the fish are often found in large schools on the shoals of clear waters emptying into the Mississippi.

Regardless of which of the basses the angler is after, he should keep in mind that the fish are primarily open-water fish; they travel in schools and are very mobile. The real challenge is locating the fish. Trolling is one method of doing so, and once the school is located, the boat should be anchored and the school worked thoroughly.

Because the true basses are often hard to locate in the big bodies of water they love, the new electronic fish-finders have become valuable items of the true bass angler's tackle.

Chapter 5
MANAGEMENT

The true bass, particularly striped bass, white bass and white perch, gained early prominence as commercial fishes, and the fact that they have been able to sustain heavy harvests and still flourish is a tribute to their perseverance. However, as interest in angling developed in America, the sporting qualities of the fish came into focus. This new interest in the fish created a serious conflict that has often tested the skills of fishery managers and law enforcement officers alike.

Management of the true basses takes two approaches. One, and perhaps the most difficult, deals with the protection of the fish from overharvesting by commercial fishermen. It requires a delicate balancing of the rights of both the commercial fishermen and sportsmen in this valuable resource, which when properly managed can often serve the needs of both. The other approach is mostly limited to freshwater habitat and deals with the rearing and introduction of the fish to new waters and their management as a sport species. Except for the commercial netting of white bass in the Great Lakes, there is little or no commercial fishing in fresh water.

The true basses are prolific, hardy, adaptable and reasonably tolerant of polluted waters. These characteristics lend themselves to good fishery management.

Early fisheries management was a simple science, involving little more than capturing fish in one body of water and transferring them to another. The need for an additional species in the strange waters was often debatable. Too often the other bodies of water were already highly productive of other kinds of fish. The competition was unwelcome. A good example of irresponsible stocking of fish is the carp, a European fish that America could have gotten along well without.

On the other hand, the introduction of new fish to strange waters has had its bright spots. The introduction of the striped bass to the waters of the Pacific, primarily along the coast of California, has become a landmark in American fisheries management.

As early as 1879, the striped bass had established itself as a fine sporting fish in Atlantic coastal waters. I am not sure how its fame spread to California, but about this time a modest shipment of 132 small stripers was taken from the Navesink River in New Jersey, transported by rail to California, and released near Martinez. Three years later, in 1882, another 300 bass were released in lower Suisun Bay.

Whether both or only one of these releases survived is not known, but within a few years large numbers of striped bass were being caught in California waters. And by the fabulous Gay Nineties era, tasty bass were being sold in San Francisco markets.

The commercial catch grew to over a million pounds a year before it was outlawed in 1935 in favor of sport fishing. Today California anglers take over 750,000 stripers annually, and smaller catches are made all along the West Coast as far north as Oregon.

Probably the most successful introduction of fish to new waters ever made was this release of the Atlantic striped bass in the waters of the Pacific.

However, successful though this venture was, no further attempts have been made to introduce the striped bass to salt or brackish waters. The reason is obvious. With the fish already abundant along the Atlantic Coast, and successfully established in the Pacific, there were no other American waters suitable for this anadromous fish that migrated back and forth along the coast and into tidal estuaries. The striper is essentially a cold-water fish and does not adapt to tropical or subtropical temperatures.

A good deal of effort has been exerted in trying to establish a migratory pattern of the striper along the Atlantic Coast. The Chesapeake Bay in Maryland and Virginia is considered the prime wintering and production ground for most of the Atlantic Coast striper population. These Chesapeake Bay reared fish range up the Atlantic Coast to New England and Nova Scotia. As a consequence striper management efforts practiced in these two states have a good deal of influence on the Atlantic bass populations.

Both Maryland and Virginia have established minimum-size limits on striped bass and have imposed other regulations designed to protect the brood stock.

Generally though, there is limited regulation of striped bass fishery in the Atlantic and that which exists has been obtained over stiff opposition from both commercial and sports fishermen. The big waters of the Chesapeake Bay, Hudson River, Long Island Sound and other striper hotspots make regulations difficult to enforce. However, enlightened attitudes and educational programs are beginning to bring about better cooperation on the part of anglers all along the coast.

South Carolina striped bass fishing got a shot in the arm in 1941 when the new Santee-Cooper Reservoirs started flexing their muscles with 160,000 acres of fresh water. Neither anglers nor fishery biologists realized it at the time but when the big dam was plugged, an indeterminable number of stripers were caught behind it. Fishermen in pursuit of largemouth bass and panfish checked in from time to time with a

(Top) An overabundance of white perch causes the species to become stunted because of the shortage of food. (Bottom) Inroads made by commercial fishermen cause concern to biologists charged with the management of striped bass for sports fishing.

(Top) These husky striped bass from the Santee-Cooper Reservoirs are examples of the product of good fishery management. (Bottom) Tennessee biologists have developed a hybrid bass by crossing the white bass and striped bass. Photo courtesy of Tennessee Game and Fish Commission.

striper or two on their stringers, and by 1948 the stripers began to show up in large numbers and in a wide range of sizes.

The situation puzzled biologists who had been of the opinion that striped bass, like salmon, were anadromous, spending most of their lives in salt or brackish waters, but returning to fresh water to spawn. After all, was this not a well established biological fact? No one had ever questioned it. But those South Carolina bass could not return to salt water, so the old theory was blown sky-high. The striped bass did not have to return to salt water as a part of its life cycle, after all. In fact, it was now established that the stripers were indeed completing their life cycle—spawning, living and dying in the big impounded waters of Santee-Cooper.

And so Santee-Cooper became famous for its landlocked striper fishing, and a whole new concept for the management of these hand-some bass was born. A few years later, the fish were established in Kerr Reservoir on the North Carolina-Virginia border to the north of Santee-Cooper. A hot striped bass fishery grew quickly there, and soon Tennessee, Alabama, Georgia, and many other southern and western states were experimenting with the striper in their own waters.

Striper fry can be hatchery-reared and many states are doing so. Fishery men in both North Carolina and Virginia have been very suc-cessful in this respect, and have for a number of years been engaged in the trading of striper fry for muskie, northern pike and other species which they wanted to introduce to their home waters. Many states, desirous of promoting the striper in their waters, have turned to Vir-ginia and the two Carolinas for eggs and fry which they have reared to release size in their own facilities.

The striped bass has proven itself very adaptable to hatchery production.

A good deal of effort has also been devoted to the management of the white bass, also a highly prolific fish that promises new horizons in big reservoir angling. They seem to be ideally suited to such waters, and many state fishery departments have taken advantage of this. The fe-male white bass will deposit from half a million to almost a million eggs. The fish are gregarious, prolific, grow rapidly and mature early. Their life-span is short. Both size and creel limits are liberal—where they exist at all; white basses can withstand tremendous fishing pressure.

As was the case with the striper, early interest in the white bass focused on its qualities as a food fish. As early as 1830, the commercial catch of Lake Erie fishermen was made up almost entirely of white bass. During the next few years an estimated 10 tons of white bass were thrown overboard annually because the market would not absorb addi-tional fish. Since that time, population levels have bounced about from one year to another.

(Top) Striped bass and white bass have proved themselves adaptable to life in the big impoundments. (Bottom) Striper hatchery of the Virginia Commission of Game and Inland Fisheries.

The white bass feeds mostly on small fish, including its own, and this quality has made the fish a natural for controlling threadfin and gizzard shad populations in the large reservoirs.

Old rivermen in Ohio insisted that the migratory fish decreased in great abundance immediately following the installation of dams on the Ohio River.

Except for the regulation of the commercial catch in a few states and rather generous seasons, creel and size limits, most management effort has been directed toward the introduction of the white bass to new and suitable waters. This trend has been highly successful and as a result the fish is now found in many parts of the United States—particularly in the South and West—far from its original midwest range.

Generally, fishery managers seek large bodies of water with good feeder streams for their white bass releases. Bass prefer the feeder streams for their spawning activities, though they can spawn in shoal or shallow areas. However, moving waters are needed to keep the eggs suspended above the bottom.

White bass can be produced successfully in hatcheries but this approach is not a popular one. The white bass is extremely prolific and obtaining the needed brood stock for introduction to new waters is rarely a problem. Once the fish adapt to new waters, further introductions are rarely necessary.

Tennessee and South Carolina biologists have collaborated in an interesting new experiment to produce a hybrid between the white and striped bass. This produces an interesting fish and one with good sporting qualities. White bass fishing methods work for the hybrid, a powerful fighter and excellent eating. Whether this program will be expanded by these states and eventually introduced to others is unknown at the present. The hybrid is a larger fish than the white bass, but there is some feeling that the successful development of striped bass fishing will curtail further interest in the hybrid.

Like the striped and white basses, the little white perch has long been a popular commercial fish and a delicacy on the American dinner table. It too has been harvested heavily by commercial fishermen all along the Atlantic Coast. Fortunately, the white perch can sustain heavy harvests and still hold its own. Little or no restrictions have been placed on commercial fishing for white perch.

While fishing pressure is a serious problem among many species of game fish, this is not the case with the white perch. On the contrary, controlling its numbers is often a problem. Introduced indiscriminately to small freshwater ponds and lakes, it can quickly become overpopulated, depriving more desirable game fish of food, and eventually becoming stunted itself. Usually the only solution is to drain or poison the water, remove all fish including the white perch, and start over again.

In the South where the perch is primarily a fish of the big salt and brackish waters, management of the species is extremely difficult and for the most part totally unnecessary. Given a reasonable chance—clean waters and a chance to spawn each spring—the white perch can more than hold its own. While overpopulation does occur, it is rarely a problem in the big southern waters, and one for which biologists have no answer, should it arise. It is in New England that the white perch thrives primarily in fresh water, and here overpopulation is a problem. Biologists discourage stocking white perch except under controlled conditions and in fact attempt to keep the fish out of good salmon and trout waters. However, they are not always successful.

To my knowledge there have been no attempts to hatchery-produce white perch, and there is really no reason to do so. The fish are readily available from natural rearing waters. For the most part the stocking of white perch has been limited to waters within their natural range, though introductions have been made as far west as Nebraska.

Very little management effort has been directed toward the yellow bass, the fourth member of the true bass family. The fish is relatively unimportant from both commercial and sporting standpoints.

There has been limited stocking of the fish within its natural range, but otherwise very little attention has been given to the yellow bass. In time this could change. The yellow bass has the same general characteristics that have attracted the angler's attention to the white and striped bass. As interest in these two more popular basses continues to grow, fishery managers might well take a second look at the yellow bass.

The fact that the true basses seem to have accepted man's manipulation of their destiny bids well for the future of these fish. Certainly for the present there seems to be no limit to the kind and quality of angling they can afford. With good management it would seem that most waters in America are suitable for at least one of the true basses.

Chapter 6

FISHING METHODS

Even the big striped bass is an inshore fish so none of the true basses fit into the offshore fishing picture. Otherwise there is no form of angling in which the true basses cannot play an interesting and important part.

Let us take the dry-fly angler for example, the purist of the pure. He may consider the white perch beneath his dignity, but this little bass is an extremely clean fish and inch for inch or ounce for ounce he will fight on even terms with the brook trout. The dry-fly angler can catch a late afternoon rise of white perch on some northern lake and have a ball while the fish are feeding. These perch will not be large, but neither are native brook trout taken from tiny headwaters streams.

First let us discuss some common characteristics of the four fish, characteristics which should permit the angler to move from one species to another and generally employ the same fishing tactics.

All of the basses travel in schools much of the year, and once the angler locates them he can usually concentrate on the school and often fill his limit without moving. To locate the schools he may have to resort to trolling at various depths and over a variety of water. Today, however, electronic fish-finders eliminate much of the guessing and reduce the time required to locate the fish. Since the fish generally prefer open water and big water the employment of the fish-finding devices can be used with a high degree of success.

None of the basses are surface-feeders in the sense that the largemouth or smallmouth bass are. Schools of baitfish may draw them to the top, but generally the angler should resort to underwater lures or baits in his search for the basses. They may be in the shallows at certain times of the year, but even then the angler will be more successful if he fishes near the bottom.

The larger members of the true bass family all feed on small minnows or baitfish, and the angler will not go wrong when he uses this kind of bait, regardless of whether he is fishing for big stripers or jumbo white perch. Worms are also popular natural baits for all four fish, though more so for stripers and white perch than for the freshwater bass. Bloodworms will take both stripers and white perch.

Once hooked, all four fish employ much the same battle tactics. They are not jumpers and seldom break water. However, the frothy boil of a big striper rolling near the surface is a thrilling spectacle. The fish

72

are all stubborn fighters and do not give up easily, though they like to fight it out in the depths. They hit hard and the angler is rarely in doubt as to whether he has a strike as is sometimes the case with slow takers such as the walleye.

(Top) White bass can be taken in the spring by casting small spoons and bucktails. (Bottom) Striped bass anglers work a tributary run of landlocked stripers, casting to the shoreline much as they would fish for largemouth or smallmouth bass.

Trolling is a common method of angling for the four basses. Many fishermen do not like to troll, but it is effective. Many big striped bass are taken in this manner, particularly in Chesapeake Bay and other large bodies of water. White perch fishermen often troll to locate the fish and then anchor and take them by casting or fishing with natural baits. White bass anglers troll once the spawning runs are over and during periods when they cannot be located by surface activities. The serious bass fisherman will soon learn that he has to accept trolling as a part of his angling repertoire.

Bait casting, or casting plugs and spoons on a fairly short rod and a revolving spool reel, is almost a lost art, now that spinning tackle has become so firmly established in America, but it is still an effective form of fishing. In no other form of angling does the fisherman have such complete control of his lure. Pinpoint accuracy in placing the lure on target is an ideal the bait-caster can realize.

I have caught white perch on bait-casting tackle as I plugged the weedy shorelines of the Potomac River for largemouth bass, but I do not recommend bait casting for the smallest of our basses. However, it is entirely possible to use light bait-casting tackle and work small spoons and lures over white perch waters and land some good fish. Lures that imitate small baitfish should produce. And a good bait-caster could no doubt be very effective casting to surface-feeding white bass, though light spinning tackle is more popular for this kind of fishing.

Of the four basses the striper is undoubtedly the most likely quarry for the bait-caster and his tackle. In the spring and fall when the fish are working and feeding in the shallows and near the shoreline, an experienced bait-caster can have a ball casting surface or shallow swimming lures to the feeding stripers. For the heavier fish the sturdy bait-casting rod is just about ideal. It gives the angler the punch to drive home the hooks and the backbone to fight a good fish to the net. The striped bass angler should by all means consider bait-casting tackle as part of his equipment. It can even be used in the surf or off of the jetties.

Spinning tackle no doubt gets the heaviest workout of all when it comes to fishing for the true basses. It ranges from heavy surf-fishing tackle to ultralight outfits used to dunk bloodworms in the spring as the white perch make their spawning runs and fill thousands of stringers for happy anglers.

For the occasional surf-fisherman who does not get enough practice to master the conventional heavy surf-casting rod and the big revolving spool reels, spinning tackle is ideal. It is certainly heavy enough for the coastal cruising stripers and a joy to use. I have also used this type of spinning tackle for trolling from the stern of charter boats.

The white bass fisherman finds spinning tackle just about ideal. It is light, easy to master, and handles light lures well. It is just about perfect

(Top) Santee-Cooper guide baits striper hook with herring. (Bottom) A youthful angler watches his line for telltale action of a landlocked striper.

(Top) A Chesapeake Bay angler glasses the water for signs of feeding stripers. The action of gulls often leads the angler to fish. (Bottom) Santee-Cooper anglers catch small herring against grates of dam. The herring is used for striper bait.

(Top) Trolling for striped bass on Chesapeake Bay. (Bottom) White perch can often be located by trolling. Photo courtesy of Tempo Products Company.

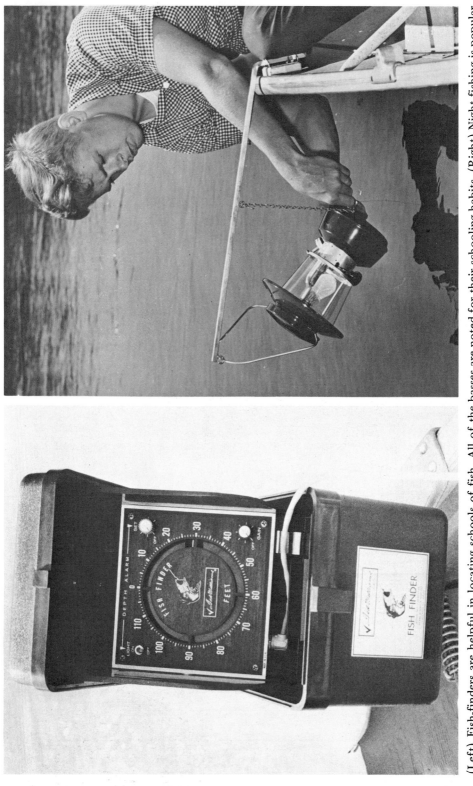

(Left) Fish-finders are helpful in locating schools of fish. All of the basses are noted for their schooling habits. (Right) Night fishing is popular for white bass. The light from the lantern attracts insects which attract small fish; they, in turn, attract the white bass. Photo courtesy of Tempo Products Company.

for casting to the "jumps." Most anglers who fish the spawning runs also use spinning tackle. It permits a soft cast that will not snap a live minnow from the hook, and is ideal for casting light jigs which spring bass fishermen find so effective. Few white bass exceed a couple of pounds and light spinning tackle makes catching them a sporting proposition. Even ultralight tackle with 4—6-pound test line can be used effectively.

I would guess that 90 percent of the white perch caught in America today are the victims of light spinning tackle. For the best sport, ultra-light outfits should be employed and 2-pound test line will catch more fish—and land them safely. The majority of white perch are caught on natural baits. Bloodworms are the most popular bait and they are usually cut into sections and fished on small hooks. Small live minnows will also take white perch and they are easy to cast on light spinning tackle.

Of course, the white perch angler can also bring into play a wide variety of small artificial lures with tiny spoons and doll flies—both good choices and easy to cast on light spinning tackle.

The fly rod probably gets its heaviest use by striper fishermen who wade the flats of tidal bays and rivers and cast bugs and streamers to feeding bass. This is top sport, pioneered by veteran anglers like Joe Brooks, and followed by expert fly-fishermen interested in new forms of angling to make use of their long, limber rods.

This is heavy tackle fishing. Rods with plenty of backbone and 9—10 feet in length are necessary to handle the big striper lures, and to drive home the hook in the mouth of the striking fish. Plenty of backbone is also needed to fight the big fish, some of which exceed 30 pounds even when taken from shallow water. A big reel is also needed to hold plenty of backing. Big stripers make long runs and the successful angler has no choice but to let his adversary have its head.

Big popping bugs are favorite lures. The angler wades slowly through the shallow water, watching for feeding fish. Once he locates them, he moves into casting range, hoping to take two or three before the fish spook and scatter. Big streamers, 4—5 inches long, are also good.

It is doubtful that the fly rod will ever get much use in fishing for white or yellow bass, though some enterprising angler might come up with an interesting technique as interest in these two fish increases.

However, the fly-rodder can certainly get plenty of action with white perch whether it be casting tiny spoons or streamers to spawning perch or dropping dainty dry flies on a broad lake when white perch dimple the surface as they rise to feed.

The white perch fisherman's fly-fishing tackle does not have to be fancy, but it should be light for the most fun. Trout tackle will serve him well. A bass bugging outfit will also work.

White perch and striped bass are sometimes taken in Chesapeake Bay on cut bait.

The white perch is a favorite of the cane-pole set. Cane-polers fish from anchored boats, from docks, or the river banks, and they catch white perch—particularly in the spring when the fish are migrating.

Finally there is the ice-fisherman, a hardy angler who bundles against the cold of a northern winter and tries to keep warm while he watches his tip-ups. Ice fishing is popular and a fast growing sport due to snowmobiles and insulated winter clothing. However, veterans have been at it for years. Of the four basses the white perch is the most likely quarry for the ice-fisherman, but abundant as it is on many inland lakes, it provides enough sport for all of its cousins. In recent seasons, some South Dakota anglers have discovered the joys of fishing through the ice for white bass in the big impoundments in that western state.

Name a form of angling and there will be a member of the true bass family waiting in the wings to provide the fishing.

Chapter 7

FISHING FOR STRIPERS

The big striped bass, a favorite of the hardy surf-fishing clan on both the Atlantic and Pacific Coasts, and popular wherever he fins the big waters he loves, has to rate as the top member of the true bass family.

While surf fishing is extremely popular where it exists, I feel that trolling takes more fish each angling season and is enjoyed by more striped bass anglers. For that reason it is dealt with first in this chapter on fishing for stripers.

There is nothing exclusive about trolling for stripers. Trolling craft range from small outboards manned by a lone angler, who keeps one hand on the motor handle and the other on the trolling rod, to expensive charter boats operated by professional fishing guides. Many expensive privately owned boats and small yachts also troll for striped bass.

Stripers are scattered much of the year and trolling was once the only way to locate the fish, but modern electronic fish-finders have eliminated this need. However, fish-finders are already being outlawed in some waters.

Stripers school in the fall, winter and spring, but scatter in the summer.

Trolling tackle is usually supplied by professional fishing guides, but the private angler has a wide choice. He should keep in mind that he may tangle with a scrappy fish and 30–40 pounds of fighting muscle, and be guided accordingly in his choice of tackle. In some waters ordinary bait-casting or spinning tackle will serve well, but in big waters such as the Chesapeake Bay or Santee-Cooper Reservoirs in South Carolina, heavy boat rods are recommended. These are reasonably sturdy rods of 5–7 feet in length and fitted with double handles—fore and aft of the reel seat. Most tackle shops or marinas in striped bass country stock them. The reel too should be heavy, and large enough to hold several hundred yards of 20–30-pound test line. A good saltwater reel, equipped with a free spool release and a star drag, will serve well for trolling for big stripers.

Striped bass are not fussy when it comes to lures, but over the years some favorites have evolved among striped bass anglers. Big bucktails are among the best. Tied on lead forms, they sink rapidly and can be fished at various depths. Bucktails weighing a half ounce to an ounce are the most popular, and they can be fished on fairly light tackle. Some anglers attach strips of yellow pork rind. Eels, both live and

(Top) A patient angler waits for a Santee-Cooper striper to take his herring bait. (Bottom) This small striped bass was taken by casting a jig along the Chesapeake Bay Bridge-Tunnel.

(Top) Big stripers do not give up easily. (Bottom) Another nice striper comes aboard.

artificial, have long been popular with striper fishermen. Spoons and plugs of various styles are also used effectively by trollers. Kerr Reservoir anglers like the Hotspot.

Trolling boats move at a slow pace and the angler adds action to his lure by jerking his line at irregular intervals to make his lure imitate a small fish darting here and there in the water.

Summertime anglers at Santee-Cooper Reservoirs find their stripers extremely deep (30—40 feet) and the troller has to use a lead core line to get his lure or bait down where the big stripers are waiting. While most anglers start trolling with approximately 100 yards of line out, they have to vary this according to the depth of the water and the speed of the boat. If they find themselves hanging up on the bottom, they have the choice of shortening their line or increasing the speed of the boat.

Trolling is an exploring proposition. The angler covers a lot of water and all kinds and depths, but generally he should be guided by the striper's preferred habitat as described in Chapter 4. Rocky shore reefs are good.

From Cape Cod, Massachusetts, south to Cape Hatteras, North Carolina, surf fishing for striped bass is a heady sport, an invigorating kind of angling that seldom produces the numbers of bass that trolling does, but a demanding sport that real enthusiasts would not trade for any kind of angling in the world.

Other hot surf-fishing spots along the Atlantic Coast include Long Island, Assateague Island and Virginia Beach. On the West Coast, the rocky shoreline from San Francisco Bay north to Coos Bay, Oregon, furnish many hours of fine striper surf fishing.

The rocky nature of the Pacific beaches makes the use of the famous beach buggy difficult, but the well equipped beach buggy is the mark of the veteran surf-fisherman along the Atlantic Coast. These often odd looking vehicles feature four-wheel drives and big balloon tires for negotiating the sandy beaches, and rod holders for a variety of rods and fish boxes for icing the catch. Some also contain sleeping accommodations.

Many makes of automobiles are converted into beach buggies. The result is an interesting vehicle which enables the angler to cruise the beaches in search of feeding fish, or water which experience tells him should yield the big oceangoing stripers. Surface disturbances and feeding gulls are two signs the angler is alert for. The veteran angler is also an expert at reading the water, watching for sloughs and cuts in offshore sandbars where the fish enter the inshore surf to feed. The angler who knows his surf is the one who will catch the stripers for he can locate his quarry. Once located, half the battle has been won as the striper is not usually difficult to entice into striking an artificial lure or natural bait. The beach buggy makes the angler mobile. A group of energetic surf-fishermen operating out of Ocean City, Maryland, say this with their name, Assateague Mobile Sportfishermen's Association—an unwieldy but descriptive one.

A thorough discourse on surf-fishing tackle goes far beyond the realm of this book, but basically there are two types in use; the long surf-fishing rod with a big revolving spool reel and the shorter spinning rod fitted with an open-face stationary spool reel. The long rod and revolving spool reel are probably still considered conventional tackle

Casting into the Atlantic surf in hopes of catching a cruising striper.

and the preference of veteran anglers. They claim this tackle permits longer and more accurate casts, and more control over a hooked fish. However, these reels are more difficult to master because of the tendency to permit the reel spool to overrun the line, causing it to double back and backlash. The spool has to be thumbed with the proper tension in order to get the longest cast and still not risk a nasty backlash. The open-face spinning reel offers the same advantages inherent in all spinning reels. It is easy to master and free of the risk of a backlash. Spinning tackle is the best choice for the occasional surf-fisherman and is gaining converts among the regulars.

Other tackle includes plenty of 25—30-pound test line, a sand spike, chest waders, a tackle bag for the variety of tools every angler needs, a rod holder to strap around the waist, a folding stool to rest upon when fishing is slow, and a good selection of lures. If natural baits are used, a knife and cutting board are necessary.

In a pinch freshwater spinning tackle or bait-casting tackle can be used for surf fishing, but it is really unsuitable for the job. Such tackle is more effective for fishing from jetties or rocky areas where the stripers will be found close to shore. These areas are popular and productive night-fishing spots.

Bait-casters find striped bass fishing productive on protected waters such as coves and sounds. These fish are usually in the pan-size class, and they offer good fishing at certain times of the year when they move into the shallow water. This occurs in the spring and fall.

Ordinary freshwater bait-casting tackle will serve fine. The type designated for bass fishing is good, and a wide variety of freshwater plugs will take the small stripers. Spoons and shallow-running plugs are dependable, but the angler should experiment until he finds what the fish favor. Bait-casters usually fish from small boats, working the shoreline, looking for rocks, vegetation, windfalls and other likely striper hangouts. A bait-casting team is a good idea; one angler paddles and handles the boat while the other fishes. They alternate so the fishing time is evenly divided.

Bait-casting tackle also gets lots of work during the spring spawning run of the landlocked stripers as they work their way up feeder streams. Plugs and spoons are good there also, but probably the most popular lure is the lead-headed jig trimmed with a yellow or white bucktail. The river bait-caster also fishes the shorelines looking for rocks, boulders, downed trees and other cover. He also works the currents and eddies, trying to place his lure where the striper lies in wait for the stream to bring him his food.

What has been said regarding the bait-caster also applies to the angler who prefers to fish with spin-casting tackle. In fact, many anglers no doubt prefer to use spin-casting tackle, fishing it the same way they would bait-casting tackle. It is fairly heavy—strong enough to handle a big fish, and it does not present the problem of a backlash.

Generally speaking, spinning tackle, that is, the open-face type, is rather light for big stripers, but it gets heavy use on pan-size fish. The angler should stay away from ultralight spinning tackle, even for pan-size fish as there is always the outside chance of tangling with a trophy fish that would be apt to snap a thin line.

The saltwater fly-rodder can have a real ball with the big striped bass when they move into the shallows to feed. The angler climbs into chest waders and moves slowly so as not to disturb the feeding fish. It is necessary for him to get fairly close, though a good fly-rod man can lay out a long line. Big popping bugs, big-brother sizes to the regular bass styles, are favorites of the striped bass angler. Big streamers, 4- or 5-inch ones, are also popular as they imitate small baitfish, a favorite food of the striper.

The saltwater fly rod must be a strong one. It must have good length, 9—10 feet, and enough backbone to handle a long line and drive a hook into the jaw of a striper.

Santee-Cooper striper anglers head out with their bait buckets full of herring.

Fly fishing for stripers, like surf fishing, is a quality sport though it will not ordinarily put the pounds of fish into the freezer that other methods will.

Natural baits—small baitfish, bloodworms, clams and other such choice tidbits of the striper's diet—probably take as many bass every season as do artificial lures. Shedder crabs and skimmer clams are favorite baits.

Fish are a staple in the striper's diet. Anglers at Santee-Cooper, where landlocked striped bass fishing has become renowned, favor the anadromous herring that migrate up the tidal rivers in the spring just as fishing for stripers hits a peak in the big reservoirs. Santee-Cooper fishing guides have perfected a method of placing a large rectangular net against the grates of the big dam and as the fish gather against it in an attempt to work back downstream, the net is raised and the fish are captured.

Herring are by no means small fish. They average 8–10 inches in length and would put up a fair fight on ultralight spinning tackle. These baitfish are hooked just in front of the dorsal fin and lowered carefully into 20–30 feet of water where they are fished just above the bottom. For the angler who can locate the fish, this is a highly productive method of bait fishing. Some anglers like to use a jumbo-size bobber and suspend their herring about 20 feet down. These bobbers are about the size of a heavyweight boxer's fist and it is quite a thrill to see one of them disappear beneath the surface; the angler knows he has a good fish on the end of his tackle.

San Francisco Bay striper anglers use live anchovies hooked to the rear of the dorsal fin. Their rig consists of a three-way swivel with a 3-foot length of leader holding a size 4 hook tied to one eye, and a 10–12-inch dropper line with a sinker on the other. California anglers like an incoming tide, but will also fish an outgoing one. The object is to fish when there is some tidal activity. The anchovy rig is bounced along the bottom and when a striper takes the bait and tightens up on the line, the angler strikes. West Coast anglers also like to let their boats drift until they locate their fish.

Drifting soft-shell crabs is a popular method of catching stripers in the Chesapeake Bay. To do this the angler anchors his boat near the edge of a grassy shallow area or other likely striper water and permits the current to carry his bait to the fish. He simply threads the crab on his hook and lets it drift freely with the current. He does not use a sinker, nor does he attempt to cast his bait. This can be a highly productive method of catching stripers.

Bloodworms are an old and established striper bait, though in recent years the big worms have become somewhat scarce and consequently expensive. There are many methods of fishing them. They can be trolled slowly, but this is expensive as the worms die quickly or are torn from the hook. Probably most are fished on the bottom or suspended just above it by anglers fishing from an anchored boat in known striper water. They can also be fished in the surf. The angler uses his regular surf-fishing tackle and casts beyond the breakers, letting his bait rest on the bottom. Hopefully, a roaming striper will pick it up.

The turbid tail waters below major striper reservoirs, such as Kerr Reservoir in North Carolina and Virginia, and Santee-Cooper Reservoirs in South Carolina, also offer an exciting form of striper fishing. The fishing is so popular at Kerr Dam that a special catwalk has been built along the side of the river just below the dam for use by anglers. From

(Top) These husky stripers were taken by trolling, a popular fishing method wherever stripers are found. (Bottom) A large boat net is needed to land big stripers.

this catwalk anglers use heavy tackle, surf-fishing tackle being popular, and cast both bucktail jigs and live and cut bait into the fast waters. The fishing is often slow, but every once in a while an angler strikes it rich and fills a good stringer. In fast water the stripers put up a good tussle.

So that is striper fishing. It ranges up the northern halves of both coasts and across the southern half of the United States. It is an ancient form of angling, but still just as exciting as it ever was, and the best thing about striper fishing is that it is growing—in interest as well as geographically. The old methods will attract new followers and the newcomers will contribute new methods to the sport. But regardless of the method employed, striper fishing is a high quality sport wherever it is practiced.

Chapter 8

FISHING FOR WHITE BASS

One September many years before I became interested in white bass as a game fish, I was fishing Dale Hollow Lake in Kentucky with my brother-in-law. After a rather long and nonproductive stretch on the big lake, we spotted a boat tied up on a small wooded island. On closer examination we discovered a tidy camp back in the trees and Jim recognized the camping anglers as neighbors from his hometown. We went ashore to visit with them.

In the course of the conversation, one veteran angler among the group told of catching a pair of nice white bass while trolling a long channel between two islands. He showed us the handsome fish, and we went back to our own angling with renewed enthusiasm. White bass probably provide the fastest freshwater fishing known.

That evening, as we gathered around the dining counter in the fishing camp restaurant, I listened while another angler told of having success-fully fished the "jumps." Listening further, I gathered he was referring to the surface ruckus caused by a school of frantic minnows or baitfish being chased by a school of white bass. Casting to the action, he had enjoyed some exciting fishing.

A number of years later the Virginia Outdoor Writers Association of which I was a member, was meeting at big Claytor Lake in southwest Virginia. It was spring in the picturesque western part of the state, and we had been lured there by reports of a good white bass spawning run in New River which feeds Claytor Lake.

Following a work session on Friday evening, we were on the lake early the next morning and in the company of several crack local an-glers who had agreed to guide the visiting writers.

George Huber (outdoor editor for the Washington *Evening Star*) and I drew a prize in Sam Turner of nearby Dublin. Sam loaded us aboard his comfortable, well equipped boat, and we headed up the lake to where the beautiful New River poured its cold waters into the reservoir. Several times en route we slowed down to talk to some of Sam's friends who were fishing from the shore.

We were on the tail end of the spawning run, Sam advised us, but the fish were still hitting. However, the action was nothing compared to what it had been about the middle of April when limit catches of 25 stripes were not unusual.

George, Sam and I spent most of the morning on the lake, trolling, casting white and yellow doll flies, and fishing with live minnows which Sam had obtained from one of his friends. As Sam had predicted our success was limited, but we learned a great deal about white bass fishing just listening to Sam and following his instructions.

White bass creels often run large. Photo courtesy of New Mexico Department of Game and Fish.

The white bass is a popular fish down in the Tennessee Valley Authority lakes which spread over so much of the "Volunteer State" countryside. And when the weather gets hot, the Tennessee angler likes to do his fishing in the cool of the evening after the hot sun has disappeared behind the hills. He fastens a gasoline lantern to the side of his boat and lets its glow flood the surface of the water. Soon insects start to gather around the light and small fish rush in to feed on the insects; then the white bass come to feed on the minnows. Tennessee anglers take them on doll flies and live bait.

It is my opinion that most of the white bass caught in the United States are taken during the annual spring spawning migrations. The flashy, silver-colored fish crowd the streams and shoal areas at that season and it is not difficult to take a quick limit—in most states white bass creel limits are liberal. During this spring fishing festival, anglers crowd the banks and feeder streams, wade the shallows or streams in chest waders or hip boots, and fish from boats of every description.

The spawning run may start anytime from late February into May, depending upon the part of the United States the fish call home. It is often cold-weather fishing, real chilblain weather when bundled-up anglers look more like northern deer hunters than fishermen. However, the bitter cold does not deter the die-hard angler who stays with it until he gets a satisfactory stringer of fish.

Most anglers use light spinning tackle for spring fishing. The fish are seldom large, and a 4-pound test line will land most of them; however, a 6-pound test line is safer and gives the angler a better chance to recover snagged lures and hooks. White and yellow jigs are perhaps the most popular artificial lures. Weights of 1/16 to 1/8 of an ounce are popular, but the angler can experiment. Many white bass anglers tie their own jigs of doll flies, using lead molds for making the bodies. Small Rapalas are good, as are small spoons and spinner-fly combinations. Any lure imitating a small minnow will take white bass, for the stripes, like all members of the true bass family, feed heavily on small minnows and baitfish.

My personal preference for fishing the spring spawning run is to slip into a pair of chest waders and hit the stream. It is the most exciting kind of fishing—much like wading a salmon river or feeling your way along the rocky bottom of a fast smallmouth bass stream.

White bass can be hunted in the sense that you locate them and then plan your attack. This is known as fishing the "jumps." It takes a fair number of bass and this method has produced several state records. It is mostly summer or fall fishing when the fast-growing white bass have added heft to their spring weights.

The angler who fishes the "jumps" can become an expert in a hurry. His approach is to cruise about a big lake in a fast boat with his eyes constantly searching the water for signs of surface-feeding fish. Schools of white bass also roam the lake in search of small baitfish. Once they locate a school, they tear into it, sending the small fish scurrying in often futile efforts to escape. The tiny fish thrash around on the surface and jump in their efforts to evade the snapping jaws of the predator fish. This activity creates the "jumps" the white bass angler is looking for.

Schools are easier to spot on calm days. The smaller fish mill around in large circular schools, while the larger fish tend to stay in smaller schools and move in "V" formations. It is not unusual to find yellow perch or crappies in white bass schools.

When a school of white bass has been located, the angler moves in quickly but carefully so as not to disturb his quarry. He must get within casting range, however. He should cast to the middle or far edge of a stationary school, but in front of a moving one. He casts into the school, hooking and landing his fish as fast as possible so he can cast again before the fish become alarmed and sound. When working his lure, he should keep it as close as possible to the surface.

(Left) A Virginia angler took this pair of white bass from the New River during an April spawning run. (Right) A pair of white bass taken during a spring spawning run.

The angler may catch only two or three bass per jump.

Once the school sounds, the show is over and the angler again starts cruising the lake in search of other schools of fish.

Light spinning tackle is the best choice for such fishing, but the angler, if he prefers, can use spin-casting or bait-casting tackle. Even the dedicated fly-rod man may catch a fish or two in this manner, but he will have difficulty getting within the limited range of his tackle, and

White bass can be taken on casting tackle.

even if he is successful in getting there, he will be lucky if he lands a fish or two. The action is simply too fast for him to work out a long line frequently enough to catch many fish. For spinning tackle I would recommend a light-action rod and reel with 6-pound test line. Actually there is no reason why the expert cannot use ultralight tackle with 2—4-pound test monofilament. This makes for sporty fishing, and it will be a rare white bass that will break even a 2-pound test line. This is usually open-water fishing and the angler has plenty of room to play his fish. However, the extra time required to land a fish on ultralight tackle will limit the number of fish he can take before the school sounds.

The same lures recommended previously for spawning-run fishing will also take white bass from the "jumps."

Night fishermen also take their fair share of white bass, particularly on the big southern lakes where the heat of the summer sun makes fishing a lake during daylight hours very uncomfortable. In addition to the tackle of his choice and a boat, the angler needs a gasoline or propane lantern, such as the one manufactured by Coleman and Company, of Wichita, Kansas.

The night angler should be familiar with the lake, a familiarity gained from fishing or boating during daylight hours. He should also have some previous knowledge of likely white bass hangouts, because it is almost impossible to locate them after dark.

Once he has reached his fishing hole, the night fisherman lowers his anchor as quietly as possible and swings his lighted lantern out over the water. He readies his fishing tackle and waits—but usually not for long. Soon the insects gather around the light and, one by one, wayward ones hit or fall on the surface of the water. Struggling on the well-lighted surface, they are easy to see from deep in the water. Baitfish (including small panfish, as well) rush in to feast on the struggling insects, and pretty soon the white bass move in to feed on the small fish.

Now the angler goes into action. He may drop a jig into the water and work it up and down until he gets a strike, or bait up with a small minnow and lower it into the well populated water around his boat. He will catch white bass—probably crappie and other bass, too. Even trout are a possibility if they inhabit the lake, but the white bass furnishes most of the action; they are the prime reason the angler is on the lake.

Night fishing is a different kind of fishing. As darkness closes in, the black of the night seems to envelop the angler and his boat. Only the bright glow of the lantern keeps it away. Before he pulls up anchor and leaves for shore, the angler should extinguish the lantern and let his eyes adjust to the darkness. He may need a flashlight to work with.

Night fishing for white bass is a fairly new form of angling, but it seems destined to grow, as the heat of the summer sun discourages many anglers from fishing big southern lakes during daylight hours.

The white bass is a very popular July fish on Pymatuning Reservoir in Pennsylvania. Here, too, night fishing is popular. During the daylight hours, bass lie near the bottom in deeper holes and are difficult to locate. But as the evening shadows lengthen over the big northern reservoir, white bass regulars begin to gather along the causeway between Espyville and the Ohio line. The popular causeway is over two miles long, and it can accommodate a lot of fishermen. Anglers fish both sides of the causeway in water averaging 12—14 feet in depth.

(Top) Jigs are popular white bass lures. Many anglers make their own. Photo courtesy of The Worth Company. (Bottom) Lantern holder permits angler to swing lantern over water while night fishing. Photo courtesy of Tempo Products Company.

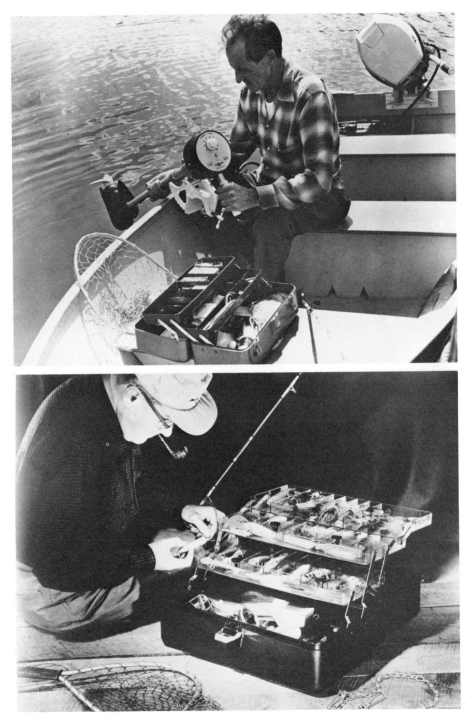

(Top) Many white bass are taken by trolling slowly. Photo courtesy of Tempo Products Company. (Bottom) Night fishing for white bass is popular during the hot summer months. Photo courtesy of Old Pal, Inc.

Most of the Pymatuning causeway anglers fish small live minnows suspended about two feet beneath the surface. A small spinner can also be effective as well as other tiny lures that resemble gizzard shad, a favorite food of the Pennsylvania white bass.

Another favorite method employed by Pymatuning anglers is to tie a 20-inch strand of leader to one of the treble hooks of a bass-size Jitterbug and fish a small streamer on the end of the leader. Reeled briskly, this rig will take white bass with fair consistency.

The white bass is not by any means an exclusive customer of anglers employing one of the previously mentioned methods. Trollers take them working slowly along channels and off of points. Many white bass are taken by anglers trolling for walleyes or other species. Down on Fontana Lake in North Carolina, smallmouth bass anglers take them in the spring while fishing live minnows 10—20 feet deep. And panfish anglers catch them on worms or cut bait.

The angler who learns to appreciate the white bass and fishes for it often enough is likely to devise a method of his own—one much more effective than any of those described in this chapter.

Chapter 9

FISHING FOR WHITE PERCH

Within its range there is probably no fish that furnishes more hours of fishing pleasure or more delicious meals than the little white perch. Youngsters, both boys and girls, cut their angling teeth on the fine little game fish, and older anglers, those too advanced in age to engage in more active angling, use them to carry their angling interests into their golden years. Campers and other outdoorsmen, primarily interested in fish for its food value, find the white perch a willing quarry and a tasty food fish. And when hot weather or other conditions send the more glamorous species into a slump, the white perch is usually around to help the angler fill the idle hours.

A trio of anglers awaits white perch action.

It is a calculated guess only, but I will hazard it anyway. The bulk of the white perch caught in America are, like their cousins the white bass, taken during the spring spawning run. During those exciting weeks in April (usually) hordes of these little fish move out of their saltwater homes—the ocean, bays, sounds, and tidal rivers—and start their annual migration up the major feeder streams in search of suitable water in which to deposit their eggs and take care of their obligation to per-

101

petuate their kind. In Virginia this can be the Potomac River, Rappa-hannock River and a number of others draining into Chesapeake Bay. Further up the Bay these restless little fish head up the mighty Susque-hanna and other prime fishing waters. Those that do not make it to the rivers seek out the shoal areas of bays and sounds and deposit their eggs.

Anglers fishing these spawning runs take perch by the thousands, sometimes hauling out stringers of several hundred fish in a single day. Such catches smack of exploitation of a valuable resource, but the white perch is so prolific that angling apparently has no adverse effect —even when practiced to an extreme.

Anglers who fish the white perch spawning runs use a variety of angling methods depending upon how sophisticated they want their fishing to be.

The great majority of white perch fishermen, however, bait fish with the old and highly reliable bloodworm. These big marine worms come from the coast of Maine where they are gathered by hand from natural rearing grounds. Labor costs are high and the cost is passed on to the angler, so bloodworms no longer are inexpensive. However, the blood-worm is a big animal when compared to the garden variety. One worm will catch a lot of perch, so the cost can be spread over a number of fish. The worm should be cut into sections, and a tiny portion used to bait the small hooks that are best for perch fishing.

All kinds of tackle perform white perch duty, but the ideal is light spinning tackle. I prefer ultralight for the greatest satisfaction in doing battle with the spunky little bass. I also like a 2- or 4-pound test line and small hooks. The veteran angler may soon tire of taking perch on worms and if he does he can tie on a spinner or small spoon and cast for the fish. They will hit hard and eagerly, though finding casting room may be a problem on some crowded perch streams or lakes.

The bait angler can choose between using a bobber to suspend his bait in the water and fishing it on the bottom, or letting it move along with the current if he is fishing a river or creek. Both methods will take fish, but it may pay to experiment.

I personally like to fish with a bobber. When fishing a stream the current moves it along and keeps the baited hook up in the current where the fish can see it. Without the bobber I am never sure whether my bait is where a fish can locate it, or whether it has rolled out of sight under a rock or log. Of course, so long as it is moving the angler has no worry, but once it stops he is in doubt. Many anglers feel, however, that a worm fished without a bobber has a more natural appearance as it rolls with the current. Perhaps they are correct, but I do not believe the white perch is that finicky when it comes to hitting a bloodworm.

Another reason I like a bobber is because it is so sensitive to the most cautious approach of a likely customer. And that moment when the bobber suddenly dips beneath the surface and disappears in the mysterious depths is to me one of the most thrilling moments in angling—whether the quarry is a white perch or some other fine fighting fish.

I believe the live bait angler (the one using small minnows, particularly) should in most instances use a bobber. He needs it to control the depth at which his minnow will swim. Otherwise, the minnow will head for the nearest crevice in a rock or boulder, or some other cover that will take it out of circulation so far as the roaming perch are concerned.

Mixed creel of white perch and big sunfish.

Worms will usually take the most white perch, but small minnows will take the larger ones. Some of the best white perch it has been my good fortune to land were taken on live minnows. I was not fishing for perch, however. Instead, I was dunking live minnows in the freshwater ponds on Cape Cod, in Massachusetts, hoping to interest some of the big chain pickerel those waters are noted for. These same waters are also prime white perch waters.

Thousands of white perch are taken on artificial lures. Probably most fall to those worked with light spinning tackle. Small spoons, spinner-fly combinations and a wide variety of other lures will take white perch. They should be fished deep in most instances, close to the bottom and around rocks and other likely white perch hangouts. The angler can pull on his chest waders or climb into a light boat or canoe and work the shoal areas of a lake or stream and have a ball with the little fish.

In Virginia the shad make their annual spring spawning run at about the same time the white perch start to spawn. As a consequence, numerous white perch are taken by shad anglers on the usual shad lures—darts and tiny spoons, or lures resembling red berries. Unfortunately, the average shad angler does not get too excited about white perch, but rather considers it a nuisance.

Bottom-fishermen in the Chesapeake Bay take a number of white perch every season. Perch are an important species in the bottom-feeding picture which includes weakfish, spot, croakers, bluefish and even a few striped bass. Party boats take them by the thousands, along with spot and the other bottom-feeding species. This method of fishing is the usual one which introduces the casual angler to white perch. Bottom fishing is not particularly exciting, but it does fill a fish box quickly, and white perch help the angler to do that.

Trolling will take white perch, but this is not a very exciting form of angling either. The fish are not large enough to furnish much sport on even light trolling tackle. Probably the most important role trolling can play in white perch fishing is to help the angler locate the fish. Since perch are school fish he can take the first one by trolling and then, with the school located, anchor his boat and catch his perch by casting artificial lures or fishing with natural baits.

Electronic fish-finders, so popular among anglers today, are an important part of the white perch angler's gear. While trolling will locate perch eventually, the fish-finder will normally be faster. The troller may be unwittingly operating at the wrong depth, while the fish-finder will locate the fish regardless of the depth at which they are feeding or schooling.

Bridge, pier, causeway and jetty fishermen take their fair share of white perch every season, and the little bass is often a favorite fish of this crew of cane-polers, hand-liners and what have you. These man-made features on our larger bodies of water seem to draw white perch for the tidbits of food they offer. As a result, fishing from them for white perch is a popular and often rewarding pastime.

Of the four members of the bass family, the white perch is the only one generally sought by ice-fishermen. Since they are abundant in the northeastern part of the United States where ice fishing is popular and productive, ice-fishermen take their share of white perch. Though ice-fishermen rarely fish specifically for any particular species, where they are abundant the white perch can be counted upon to comprise the major part of any ice-fishing catch.

The little white perch is abundant within its range, so easy to catch, so available and so tasty that it is difficult to visualize a fishing world without this smallest member of the true bass family.

Chapter 10

FISHING FOR YELLOW BASS

Because of its limited range and relatively small size, the yellow bass has never achieved much of a reputation among anglers. This is unfortunate and rather difficult to understand for the yellow bass is generally larger than the white perch and only slightly smaller than the average-size white bass. It is also a good fighting fish and delicious in the pan.

In Illinois and other midwestern states the majority of yellow bass are taken on live baits such as minnows, garden worms and night crawlers. Many are also caught on cut bait. Spinner-bait and spinner-fly combinations are also effective when trolled or fished near the bottom. Small plugs also take many yellow bass.

In shallow water, spinners, spoons, flies and popping bugs are productive and fun to fish with.

Like other bass, the yellow is a school fish and after locating a school, many anglers prefer to still-fish with minnows, worms or cut bait.

The best fishing usually comes in the spring and early summer. Then brushy areas and submerged weed beds are good. Fishing for yellow bass in the middle of the summer is usually futile, but is brisk after the water cools in the fall. However, fall fishing does not approach the productiveness of spring fishing.

The little fish is a prime prospect for some angling pioneering. The angler can equip himself with the accumulation of knowledge already assembled on the other three members of the true bass family, study the characteristics of the little yellow bass and take advantage of this angling know-how to devise means of outwitting it.

Let us give it a try.

First, the size of the fish is an important angling consideration. The yellow bass is rarely a lunker, though a few hardy specimens may grow to 5 pounds in ideal waters. The average fish lives five years or less and may reach 10 inches in length and a half pound in weight. These figures apply generally in the Midwest where the fish is most abundant. So first of all, we have a light tackle fish, even though the yellow bass is a real scrapper. Light tackle enables the angler to get the most from his sport.

Ideally, the angler should use an ultralight spinning rod and a 2-pound test line. If he happens to be fishing water having a reputation for big bass, then he may be smart to switch to 4- or 6-pound test line. However, his ultralight spinning rod and reel will still do the job. The fly-fishing enthusiast may want to substitute like weight fly tackle.

For much of the year the yellow bass is a bottom-feeder, and like the other basses it is a lover of small fish. With this much to go on, the angler should start fishing with small spinning lures that resemble little baitfish, and if possible, he should attempt to fish with lures that resemble the minnows common to his fishing waters. From this as a start he can switch to spinner-fly combinations, spoons and just about everything in his tackle box. He will eventually learn what is most effective.

Of course, if artificials do not work, he can try natural baits—minnows, worms, salamanders, crayfish and even cut bait. Normally, though, the yellow bass is not hard to please.

(Left) The yellow bass is ordinarily a big water fish. (Right) Jigs are popular lures for yellow bass. Photo courtesy of The Worth Company.

Since fishing is usually best during the spawning season, the angler is advised to do his yellow bass fishing in April or early May. At that time he can look for his quarry over the gravel bars, rocky reefs or near underwater brush. When these usual habitat features are absent, or are hard to locate, then the best maneuver is to troll slowly with the lure close to the bottom until a school is located. Again, it pays to experiment, switching lures until the quarry's choice is established. Once the school is located the angler can continue to troll back and forth across the productive water, or if he prefers he can carefully lower his anchor so as not to frighten the fish—and cast.

The yellow bass, as is characteristic of the breed, hits hard and fights stubbornly. Light spinning or fly-fishing tackle brings out the best in him. The fish makes long determined runs, though it does not jump or normally break water. One may occasionally roll near the surface.

While the spring spawning season is the prime time to fish for yellow bass, early fall can also be good. The fishing is seldom good in the dead of winter.

Like its relatives, the yellow bass is by preference a big-water fish. As a consequence, the angler should seek him in the larger midwestern rivers, their backwaters and adjoining bottom-land lakes and larger tributaries. For example, both the Mississippi and Illinois Rivers are considered prime yellow bass waters.

Within their range yellow bass also spill over into less suitable waters. Look for them in natural lakes in the general area of large rivers. In addition, try nearby farm ponds, city reservoirs and large artificial impoundments. In the spring, particularly, it is fun to explore the smaller tributaries of the big bass rivers. By nature I am a small-stream or headwaters angler; I like to poke my way slowly up a small winding stream in search of small pockets of angling gold. While the yellow bass prefers big waters, the migratory urge that comes with the spawning season will send a few up the smaller waters. And one of the most delightful things about such a stream is that the angler usually has it completely to himself.

Anglers and fishery managers still have much to learn about the yellow bass. Colored a bright yellow and streaked with dark lateral lines, the fish is truly handsome, and its jarring strike and fighting ability put it in the game fish class. Add its appeal hot from the pan and you have all of the ingredients of a true game fish.

All the yellow bass needs is time to catch up.

Chapter 11

ICE FISHING

In most waters the striper is considered a cold-weather fish. However, it also likes large salt or brackish waters that rarely freeze; and even when such waters do freeze, they seldom develop ice thick enough to support ice-fishermen. To a less extent the same applies to the white and yellow bass, though in recent years South Dakota anglers have been taking white bass through the ice of the big Missouri impoundments. Both the white and yellow bass are strictly freshwater fish, but in much of their range they live in large bodies of water that rarely freeze completely. Since these two members of the true bass family are not particularly active in the dead of winter, they are promising ice-fishing prospects only in limited areas.

This process of elimination leaves us with the white perch. Fortunately, the little white perch is a favorite fish of the growing army of ice-fishing anglers.

It is mid-July as I write this, and Virginia is in the midst of one of the longest heat waves on record. Thoughts of frozen lakes and snow-covered hills smack of dreamland. A discussion of ice fishing takes on a hollow tone and seemingly should be left for a later date, but it is time for that chapter of the book. So here goes.

Ice fishing has become one of our most popular winter sports—one all members of a family can enjoy, though this is not always the case. Many still feel the cold surface of an ice-clad lake is something only the hardy should expose themselves to. This image of ice fishing is gradually disappearing, however.

Tip-ups, ice spuds and red flags are by no means new to fishing in America. It was back in the mid-'30's, depression years in America, when a thirst for angling knowledge led me to outdoor books and magazines. In those years, economically bleak, but rich for a youngster just starting an outdoor career, a Boston publisher issued two excellent little outdoor magazines: *Hunting and Fishing* and *National Sportsman.* They sold for a nickel per copy and I still have several in my library. I have learned a good deal from those dog-eared magazines. Here I first read of ice fishing, a sport unknown in the relatively mild climate of my native area in central Virginia. Tip-ups, spuds and red flags were popular even then during long New England winters.

A number of things have contributed to the healthy growth of ice fishing in the United States. Much of it is psychological. A young

An ice-fisherman awaits action.

generation of anglers has overcome the fear of solid ice and suddenly realized that a snowy, ice-clad outdoors can be just as attractive as the balmy days of summer. Modern outdoor equipment has played a role also. Light down-filled clothing and well insulated boots make life in the outdoors more pleasant on a winter day when the temperature is well below freezing. Modern camping equipment such as tents that can be erected without stakes, folding chairs and efficient portable heaters make ice fishing more appealing. Ice fishing gives the owners of such equipment an opportunity to get additional mileage from their investment. And of course there are portable ice shanties built just for the ice-fisherman.

The modern snowmobile that permits the angler to move quickly over a lake or river is also a big factor in the growing popularity of winter fishing.

Because of its abundance in New England, the white perch has long been a favorite of ice-fishermen in that area. Ice fishing is seldom a specialized sport to the extent that the angler fishes specifically for a certain species. However, the white perch is an important part of the ice-fishing creel that includes pickerel, yellow perch and various panfish.

The white bass adds variety to the ice-fishing catches in the Midwest, but it is not considered an important species by ice-fishermen. For one thing it is not a heavy winter-feeder. Nor is the yellow bass a particularly important ice-fishing quarry in the Midwest.

The white perch retreats to deeper water in the winter, but the angler will find his quarry living in generally the same areas of a lake in the winter as he found them during the summer months. Only during the spring spawning season does the perch leave its favorite spots. Many ice-fishermen like to fish fairly close to shore where they can build warming fires (on shore), and keep warm while watching their tip-ups. Except for sparse vegetation in the winter, there is not much seasonal change in the average lake.

The ice-fisherman should use a good deal of care in selecting his fishing waters. Chopping the necessary number of holes in the ice is a chore that will make the angler reluctant to move should the first choice be a poor one. However, once he catches a fish, he can be reasonably sure he has made a good choice as white perch live in schools and other good catches should follow the first one. Finding the fish is a major factor in the ice-fisherman's success. Once that is accomplished, he has his fishing grounds and can usually make repeated successful trips throughout the ice-fishing season. The same holes will serve for many trips, though they will frequently have to be cleaned of new ice.

The ice-fisherman's tackle can be simple and inexpensive. At the minimum he needs a crude ice spud, a heavy crowbar-like tool with a straight cutting edge on the bottom for chopping holes in the ice; an ax is a poor substitute, though a chain saw will do a reasonably good job. Ice augers are an improvement and the more expensive ones are powered by small gasoline motors. They speed up the hole-cutting process considerably.

Once the angler has cut his first hole, he may set his tip-up or ice-fishing rig for possible action while he cuts additional holes. Though the number of holes is limited by law in many states, the angler should not chop more holes than he will be able to properly attend. In strange waters, he may want to chop only one or two so he can test the fishing before expanding his tip-ups.

Thickness of the ice is a major safety consideration. It should be at least 4—6 inches thick to support an angler, his party and their tackle. He should not drive his car on the ice unless it is considerably thicker. Local people, familiar with ice conditions on a lake or river, should be consulted.

The white perch is a favorite of the ice-fishing clan.

For protection from the icy blasts of wind that sweep frozen lakes, some form of shelter is needed. At the minimum, it may be only a sheet of canvas on the windward side of the fishing holes to serve as a windbreak. More elaborate ice shanties include tents and shanties built specifically for ice fishing, complete with bunks, chairs, and heating facilities. Even the angler hiding from the wind behind a piece of stretched canvas will welcome some type of heater. There are many small portable gas heaters on the market that will serve this purpose.

Ice fishing can be a fast sport that keeps the angler hopping from one hole to another. There can also be lulls, or long periods of inactivity. During such slow periods there is little the angler can do except be patient and wait—or eventually move to another location. He will move around to keep his blood circulating but sooner or later a seat of some kind will be tempting. Bare ice makes a poor seat. The seat may be a crude sled on which the equipment is hauled to the fishing grounds. Many anglers build their own sleds and include a cushioned seat of some kind. Those who like more comfort take folding stools or beach chairs. The only criterion is the degree of comfort the angler needs or seeks.

The transportation of tackle is a consideration. Of course, if the angler drives his automobile or uses a snowmobile there is no problem, but in the absence of one of these modes of transportation he needs some type of sled to haul his gear. It may be a conventional sled fitted with towrope, though the more exacting angler will want something built more specifically for his needs—fitted with a seat, for example, or a box for holding and transporting his catch.

Tackle runs a wide gamut of styles and types. The casual angler may use his open-water spinning or casting tackle and fish through the ice in much the same manner as he would in open water. Others use conventional open-water tackle to jig special artificial lures designed for such fishing.

The basic item of ice-fishing tackle is the tip-up. Many anglers make their own. It consists of a crude reel, line, terminal tackle such as weights and hooks, and an easy-to-trip flag that signals when a fish hits. The trigger of the tip-up is set heavily enough to hold the line in place, but lightly enough to be tripped by the fish. The line flows freely from the spool but the angler, having been warned by the tripped flag, races to the hole to play the fish. He may play the fish hand-over-hand, though some anglers attach their reels to stubby rods with which they play the fish.

Other ice-fishing tackle includes stubby ice-fishing rods, jigs, whips and jacks. Ice-fishermen are an ingenious group and usually gadget-conscious. Once in a while the weather gets too severe even for the ice-fisherman and when it does, he is likely to be busy in his snug workshop or basement, fashioning new tip-ups, crude reels, a new seat for his ice-fishing sled or anything else functional to the art of ice fishing.

Most ice-fishermen forgo the use of a bobber but if live minnows are the bait, a bobber may be necessary to prevent the minnow from tripping the flag.

Miscellaneous items of equipment include an ice dipper to keep the holes from freezing over, a minnow pail if live minnows are used and a small dip net for removing the minnows from the pail. Sinkers of various weights will be needed to keep the bait down where the fish are feeding.

The ice-fisherman does not have much room in which to play his fish, so a fairly heavy line is recommended. Monofilament in the 8—10-pound test class is satisfactory for white perch and others of that size, but in waters frequented by heavier fish, 15—20-pound test line is a good safety factor. Sharp ice near the edge of the hole is likely to fray the line so it should be checked periodically.

Modern outdoor clothing offers the ice-fisherman a wide choice of cold-weather garments. The average outdoorsman probably already has clothing which is perfectly satisfactory. Since the feet and hands are the most vulnerable to frigid weather, well-insulated boots, heavy socks, and good gloves or mittens are essential items of clothing. The angler should also dress in layers so he can peel off excess clothing or put it on as the variable temperatures dictate.

Only time and future fishing seasons will determine how important ice fishing will become in the life of the true bass angler, but in the meantime, the angler who has access to an ice-covered white perch lake is fortunate, indeed.

Chapter 12

THE WEATHER

When the maples start to bud in the spring and white perch, responding to an instinct as old as time, begin their migratory spawning run up the major Atlantic tidal rivers, or white bass, yielding to the same restless urge, head up the major tributaries of big inland lakes, there is probably no weather condition possible that will stop them from hitting the angler's offering. Spring rains may create flood conditions, making such waters impossible to fish, and late winter blizzards or unseasonable weather may drive the angler home, but those who are hardy enough to battle the elements will probably catch white bass or white perch.

Several kinds of weather are unappealing to me personally—whether the fish are hitting or not. I have no objection to fishing in a snowstorm, nor on a mildly rainy day. In fact, I find such conditions different, exciting, and frequently productive. I also find that such weather conditions thin out the crowds, making fishing a more enjoyable outing.

Much of our true bass fishing is done on large bodies of water; fishing them can be dangerous on windy days. Strong winds can kick up heavy seas on larger rivers, lakes or bays, and it is no fun to fish while jockeying a bouncing boat. I also dislike extremely hot weather. The shimmering surface of a big body of water on a hot summer day can cause much discomfort.

Except for such conditions there are few weather quirks that would cause me to desert a productive body of fishing water.

After many years of skepticism I have become a firm believer in the effects of the solunar system on the feeding habits of fish and game. Numerous experiences in the fields and woods and on the waters convince me that there are peak periods during each day when fish and game feed or move about. These peak periods do not always come during the accepted early morning or late afternoon prime time for fishing or hunting.

Based on personal experiences, I have become an addict of the famous Solunar Tables originated by the late John Alden Knight and now published by the Knight family. Using a carefully guarded family secret, these tables attempt to pinpoint the periods each day when fish or game will be most active.

Too many anglers have to fish when they can find the time, and as a consequence do not pay much attention to such tables—or even the

(Top) Santee-Cooper guide prepares to net a striper on a warm spring day. (Bottom) Striper fishing can be a cold weather sport in the fall and winter and this party of Chesapeake Bay anglers dresses accordingly.

local weatherman, for that matter. The Solunar Tables are published annually, however, and the angler can use them in planning his outings.

The forecasts of the local weather station are extremely helpful—and reasonably accurate when limited to a period of four or five days. The bass angler should develop the habit of checking these forecasts. Tide tables are also helpful for the white perch and striped bass angler. The low and high tides are critical periods in tidal water fishing. The angler should take them into consideration when planning his jaunts for bass or perch.

There is probably no angler in the business more subject to the whims of the weather than the surf-fisherman. The word "surf" is the key to his problems; he needs a certain amount of surf to fish, but it should be neither too heavy nor too light. A heavy surf is dangerous—filled with strong and treacherous currents. It is also hard to fish, often flinging the angler's weighted rig back on the beach. On the other hand, a dead sea (one devoid of surf) is too lifeless to attract fish into surf-fishing waters.

So the surf angler needs surf—enough to keep the rich marine life along the shoal areas and in the sloughs and cuts stirring and on the move. This kind of surf is a signal to the striper that there is food to be had, and he moves in for the feed.

While both the white perch and striped bass are considered cold-weather fish, this does not necessarily mean that they feed only during the cold spells or abnormally cold weather. The implication concerns the season of the year—usually spring and fall or early winter. Within these seasons of cool or cold weather I frankly do not believe that routine weather changes have much to do with the fishing. The reason is simple. These fish normally live in such large bodies of water that they are practically immune to temporary changes of weather. Water is a great neutralizer of sudden changes in air temperature.

In extremely cold weather the fish may seek the shallows for warmth or in extremely hot weather they may seek the depths, moving into shallow water late in the day or during the night to feed.

Extremely high winds that kick up heavy seas and roil the shoal areas may drive both bass and perch from them. In my part of the country a strong northeast wind that persists for several days can put a damper on the fishing and most fishing guides recognize this. Hurricane weather can do the same, making large bodies of water not only dangerous to be afloat on, but also poor for fishing. Several years ago Hurricane Agnes killed a planned trip on Virginia's Rappahannock River for a friend and me. The fish had been hitting well, but the violent weather ended it all for several days.

White bass, avid surface-feeders in the summer, do not seem to be bothered by hot or humid weather, though southern anglers fish for them under the coolness of darkness.

(Top) The weather—particularly the wind—is important to the surf-fisherman. (Bottom) White bass fishermen dressed for the cold weather that often greets them when they fish the April spawning run.

Every good angler keeps an eye on the weather. He learns to read the clouds and cloud formations, the sunset and sunrise, and he knows that a ring around the moon spells foul weather. Regardless of the effect weather may have on his fishing, he keeps it in mind. He listens to the radio weather reports, reads them in the paper, and plans his fishing accordingly.

The weather is important to the bass angler, but moderate changes in the weather probably have little effect on his fishing fortunes.

This Chesapeake Bay striper was taken on a warm summer day—not the best striper fishing weather.

Chapter 13

THE ANGLER'S CLOTHING

When buying clothing the angler should keep several things in mind. Comfort is of prime importance, of course. However, the angler's clothing should also be neat in appearance, for this adds to his sense of well-being. If he is properly attired the angler will feel more at ease with his fellow anglers and other people he encounters on a fishing trip. Finally, his clothing should be inconspicuous so as to blend as much as possible with his surroundings. This is of particular importance when fishing clear, shallow water where the angler has to avoid spooking the fish. This is a consideration that is normally of more importance in other kinds of fishing (trout fishing, for example) but occasionally it becomes important among bass fishermen, too.

Let us talk about comfort first; it is the prime consideration here. Comfort includes protection from extremes of weather (cold and hot), a proper fit so the clothing will neither bind nor bag, and the necessary pockets for a wide variety of angling items.

To achieve inconspicuousness the angler should give consideration to the type of surroundings in which he will be fishing. If he is fishing a large body of deep water as is often the case in bass fishing, the color or pattern of his clothing is of no consequence, and he is free to dress according to his whim for color and style.

The fisherman who gives attention to his appearance is creating a favorable image of the angler. This is important to the continued acceptance of fishing. The costume is an important part of every sport and angling is no exception. Fortunately, today's manufacturers have provided the angler with a wide choice of attractive clothing and there is no excuse for looking shabby.

With these thoughts in mind let us dress the angler from the skin out.

There is no more important item of clothing than the underwear. Since most bass angling is done in relatively mild weather the angler is likely to forgo insulated or other heavy underwear. My personal choice for spring, summer and fall wear is light cotton two-piece underwear—boxer type shorts that fit snugly, but do not bind, and cotton T-shirts that cover the armpits. I learned to appreciate this kind of underwear during World War II while with the Marines in the tropical Pacific. The T-shirt absorbs perspiration, preventing chafing under the arms and also protecting the outer clothing from salty perspiration.

For cold-weather fishing I like snug fitting insulated underwear. The fishnet style that permits the body heat to circulate is good, but any form fitting kind will be satisfactory. I prefer this over the more bulky down-filled type because it wears better under the outer clothing. Of course, if the weather is likely to change dramatically during the day the angler may prefer the quilted style for the simple reason that it looks better should he feel it necessary to strip down to his underwear to cope with the climbing temperature.

A belt around the surf-fisherman's waist keeps out a deluge of water should he fall.

In the normal dressing process the socks follow the underwear. Wool socks are warm and they absorb perspiration, keeping the feet dry. Dry feet are usually warm feet, and this is important. Since pure wool does not wear well and has a tendency to scratch, I prefer a combination of wool and nylon. For most bass fishing, particularly that done from a boat, athletic style ankle-length socks are fine. However, if the angler plans to wear hip boots or chest waders, ankle-length socks are inadvisable because they work down in the boot and bunch up under the instep. For waders or boots, knee-length socks held in place by elastic supporters are much better. I personally like knee-length hunting socks with elastic tops that fit snugly below the knee.

Shoes are an important consideration in any type of outdoor activity. Nothing can spoil a trip more quickly than wet or uncomfortable feet. For fishing from a boat I find ordinary rubber-soled sneakers ideal. They are light and comfortable and provide good traction in a slippery boat. They are also fine for wear around boat docks, marinas, etc., and dry quickly. They are equally as good for fishing from a canoe as from a charter boat on Chesapeake Bay.

For fishing the surf or wading a feeder stream thick with spawning white bass I like chest waders. They are an absolute necessity for surf fishing, and much better than ordinary hip boots for river fishing. The angler should wear a belt over his waders, and the better ones on the market have belt loops. The belt serves a number of purposes. As a safety factor, it draws the waders tightly against the body and keeps out the water should the angler fall. It is also handy for carrying a gaff, landing net, knife or other items of use to the surf-fisherman—items he likes to keep at his fingertips.

The angler's shirt should be roomy and comfortable. It should be large enough to fit comfortably over quilted underwear if this becomes necessary for warmth. It should also have long sleeves and a wide collar. Even for summer wear, long sleeves are recommended for protection from sunburn and insects. When turned up, the collar protects the neck and provides added warmth in cold weather. The angler should insist upon big pockets with button-down flaps; shirt pockets are handy for carrying small personal items such as film, cigarettes and matches. The button-down flaps prevent the loss of these items when the angler bends over to net or gaff a fish or tie a shoestring.

For winter wear, the shirt should be of wool or similar fabric, and for summer use, light cotton is fine. Cotton flannel is good between-seasons weight. The shirt should have a long tail that covers the hips for extra warmth in the winter and fits snugly in the trousers.

Trousers should have deep, roomy pockets, and at least one hip pocket should have a button-down flap to protect the billfold. The belt loops should be large enough for a wide outdoor style belt. The season will determine the weight and kind of fabric, but it should be tough and long wearing as trousers receive considerable punishment in the course of a season of fishing. Trousers to be worn under waders or hip boots should have tabs on the bottom of the legs so they can be tightened around the ankles to keep them from working up the legs. For normal wear with sneakers or ankle-height shoes, the trouser legs should meet the tops of the sneakers. If they are longer, they impede the active angler as he scrambles about in a day of fishing.

The angler's belt should be wide and fitted with a healthy size buckle. This type of belt has an outdoor appearance and is excellent for carrying a belt knife, sunglasses, etc.

A broad-brimmed hat protects the face from sun and rain.

The angler is now dressed. The clothing worn other than what has been described depends to a large extent upon the weather. For spring and summer fishing nothing else may be needed. However, he should pack some kind of rain gear with his tackle. This can be extremely lightweight material consisting of a pair of rain pants with a drawstring top and a hooded rain shirt. In the early spring or in the fall when the temperatures may drop suddenly, he should carry a light jacket. This, too, can be easily packed with his tackle.

Almost any kind of outdoor jacket will be adequate for the boat or bank fisherman. Hunting and ski jackets serve well. However, the wading angler needs a fishing vest or jacket—one with many pockets and possibly a built-in creel. The better fishing jackets are wind- and waterproof. When worn over insulated underwear and a wool shirt, they provide adequate warmth for all but the coldest days.

The angler's hat or cap should shade his eyes and protect his neck. The ordinary baseball style cap worn by so many anglers does a good job of shading the eyes, but it does not protect the neck. And if the angler should get caught in a downpour the water pours down his neck. Battered felt hats with wide brims make good fishing hats, though they may be uncomfortable in warm weather. The summer cap or hat should be well ventilated. Wool is fine for winter wear. A stocking cap is extremely warm and comfortable and some have narrow brims.

For winter fishing, gloves are needed to protect the hands. They should be of the feel type—fingertips of tough, but thin material that permits the angler to retain the sensitive touch of his fingers, but still adequate for protection from the cold. I like tight-fitting, elastic cuffs that slide under the sleeves of my jacket.

While not considered clothing, sunglasses should be a part of every angler's equipment. When not in use, they can be carried in a belt case. They provide protection from the glare of the water or ice, and aid the eyes in penetrating the water.

The well-dressed angler is a more comfortable, happier one and usually more successful.

Chapter 14

CARE FOR THE CATCH

Americans have a reputation for being poor fish eaters. This is unfortunate because of the resulting waste of a valuable resource. Fish are rich in protein and other nutrients, and the average American would be a healthier individual if he included fish in his diet more frequently.

With the wide variety of fish found in America and their relative abundance when compared with other wildlife resources, there is no plausible excuse for fish not becoming a more frequent dish on the American table. Many anglers refuse to eat their own catches and have trouble giving them away.

The basses are among our most popular table fish and because they are so abundant the angler often finds himself with more than he can handle. Properly cared for and dressed, they can be shared with neighbors—many do not fish but do enjoy a good fish meal.

Care for the catch starts the moment the fish is removed from the hook. In fact, this can be one of the most critical moments in transforming a fine game fish into a tasty meal.

The quicker the fish is prepared for the table, the better it will taste. This is one of the reasons shore lunches are so popular on angling expeditions. The luncheon fish are prepared from the morning's catch, and most are just several hours out of the water. Of course, it is not always practical for the angler to remove his fish from the hook and cook it immediately.

Since most of the bass are caught in the spring, fall, or winter, the angler has an ally in the weather. About the only exception comes in the summer when white bass are taken by fishing the "jumps."

Many anglers store ice chests in their boats and place their catch on ice the moment it is removed from the hook. Ideally, the fish should be gutted and the gills removed before icing. Few anglers go to this trouble, however. Instead of dropping the fish on the ice, one on top of the other, the angler should attempt to spread them out in the chest so that ice separates them. Fish handled in this manner will provide excellent table fare later on.

Stringers are more common than ice chests in the average fishing boat. However, there are several practices that should be avoided if a stringer of fish is to arrive home in the best condition. Stringing the fish through the gills is one of them. Strung through both lips, fish will live for a long time. This, of course, reduces the time they have to be iced.

I personally prefer wire stringers with individual snaps for each fish. The better stringers have sliding loops. They permit the angler to string his fish without removing the stringer from the water. However,

(Top) Care for the catch starts as soon as the fish is removed from the hook. (Bottom) These stripers would fare better if they were placed on ice with ice separating the individual fish.

stringers with stationary loops are satisfactory. The angler should avoid the ordinary cord stringer on which the fish are strung one on top of the other by running the cord through the gills.

When the surface water is cool, as it usually is in the spring, a regular length short stringer which keeps the fish near the surface is satisfactory. However, in the summer when the surface water gets warm, the fish should be strung deep where the water is cool. This requires a long stringer. A strong cord or rope tied to the end of a regular length stringer will suffice.

One advantage of stringers is that the angler can delay the decision on which fish he wants to keep until he is ready to go home. The rest can be released.

With proper care, this nice catch of stripers will make several delicious meals.

Some fishing boats are equipped with live-boxes that permit the water from the lake or stream to circulate through the box. Fish placed in these boxes will stay alive for hours, providing the water is cool enough. Of course, if the water is warm, the angler faces the same problem that he does with a short stringer. The only difference is that he does not have a solution to the live-box problem.

The trip home presents problems in keeping the fish fresh and in top condition. This is particularly true if the trip is a long one—two or three days, or more.

Dry ice is one solution, but this freezes the fish solid and they must be transferred to a deep freezer immediately. Generally speaking, I prefer wet ice en route. This allows opportunity for proper preparation before freezing.

An ice chest filled with small chunks of ice mixed liberally through the catch and properly drained will do an excellent job of getting a prize catch home in prime condition. Piling the fish one on top of the other should be avoided and melting water should be drained as rapidly

A portable ice chest is excellent for transporting fish in an automobile. Photo courtesy of The Coleman Company.

as possible; a hose attached to the drain on the chest and run out of the car will serve well for this purpose. The chest should be checked frequently and the melted ice replaced.

For the best results the fish should be cleaned before being placed in the chest. This means removing the viscera, gills and the blood down each side of the backbone.

Consuming a tasty bass may not be as exciting as fighting one, but the satisfaction of a tasty fish meal is well worth the extra care.

Chapter 15

CLEANING AND COOKING

Fish fillets are hard to beat in my cookbook, and the larger basses such as the striper and bigger white bass lend themselves to this treatment. Occasionally the lucky angler will take a white perch or yellow bass large enough to fillet, but this is the exceptional case.

Smoked fillets are a true delicacy.

To fillet a fish the angler needs a very sharp knife. Most tackle stores stock fillet knives—sharp, thin-bladed knives that are well suited for the job.

The angler stretches his fish out on some kind of cutting board and makes the first cut just behind the gill covers. He cuts all the way to the backbone and then turns his knife sideways and slices the fish along the backbone all the way to the tail. He removes the fillet and completes the job by peeling the skin from the fish. He turns the fish over and repeats the process on the other side. This gives him two choice, bone-free fillets ready for the pan. The remainder of the fish—head, backbone and stomach—go into the garbage can.

It is true that filleting wastes a certain amount of the fish, but the loss is small and the angler does not have to worry about scaling, gutting and the bones. The fillets can be frozen or iced until ready for use.

To clean a smaller bass in the conventional manner, the angler should first scale his fish. Again, he needs a cutting or cleaning board to work on. He should have a gripper of some kind to firmly clasp the tail. Working from the tail toward the head, he removes the scales by working a knife or scaler against them.

The angler can purchase both grippers and scalers in most tackle shops and they are very helpful in scaling fish. Scaling is a tedious job at the best, and the angler needs all the help he can get.

Once the fish is scaled, the head should be chopped off just behind the gill covers. However, if the angler prefers to leave the head on he can do so, but by all means the gill covers should be removed. Some anglers feel the head enhances the appearance of the fish on the platter.

With the head off or the gills removed, the angler slits the fish along the belly from throat to tail. It is then a simple matter to remove the viscera. This leaves a long line of blood along each side of the backbone. The angler should remove this by running the point of his knife along the backbone.

(Top) The makings of a tasty meal—striper and bluefish taken on same trip. (Bottom) Smaller stripers can be fried.

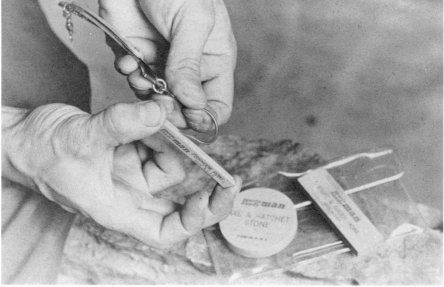

(Top) A sharp knife is needed to clean and fillet fish. (Bottom) A well-honed hook increases its efficiency. Photos courtesy of The Worth Company.

The fish is now ready for cooking or freezing. A large fish can be cut into steaks.

Outdoor cookbooks are filled with recipes for cooking bass and all other kinds of fish. However, for a starter try one of the following.

White perch, yellow bass, white bass and small stripers are excellent for frying. Fillets can also be prepared in this manner. To prepare the

Large stripers are best baked.

fish or fillet for frying, put a cupful of flour or corn meal in a paper bag, add salt and pepper, and shake each fish or fillet in the bag until it is coated completely. The fish or fillet should then be fried in butter or shortening until they are a golden brown and the flesh can be removed easily from the bones.

Many anglers like to bake larger fish such as the striper, or even a large white or yellow bass, or a truly jumbo white perch.

If the fish is a very large one, split it and place it on foil, flesh side up. To prepare the bass for the oven, brush generously with lemon juice and dot with butter. Next, salt and pepper and add a tablespoon of wine. Before placing the bass in the oven, seal the foil as tightly as possible. The oven should be preheated to 400° and the fish baked for approximately an hour. Baking time will vary slightly, depending upon the size of the fish.

The angler who learns to prepare his catch for the table will derive much additional pleasure and satisfaction from his jaunts for members of the true bass family.

Chapter 16

CHESAPEAKE BAY BRIDGE – TUNNEL STRIPERS

Glancing anxiously at Claude Rogers, I unhooked the sparkling silver-toned striped bass and slid it into the fish box. I was pleased with that school striper and hoped to land a few more like it, but I was not sure Claude shared my enthusiasm. In fact he had already racked his rod and was again glassing the broad expanse of blue Chesapeake Bay water.

Reading my host's thoughts, I knew my time over that school of hungry stripers was limited and I commenced to fish frantically.

Claude lives in Virginia Beach, close to some of the best fishing along the Atlantic Coast. He enjoys an enviable reputation as a Chesapeake Bay angler. In fact, for many years his 44-pound, 10-ounce striped bass held the Virginia state record for that popular fish. He captured his prize in the Virginia Beach surf near his home. His record was broken in 1962, and I could not help but feel he was anxious to recapture his title before another decade passed.

"Disadvantage of fishing with a champion," I mumbled to myself. Claude knows his striper fishing, but he was not interested in the scrappy 2- and 3-pounders I was having a ball with.

Finally, I reluctantly reeled in and nodded to Claude that I was willing to hunt for bigger game.

Claude had not been optimistic when I talked to him on the phone the previous day. "We have had gale winds, and right now the wind is blowing out of the northwest," he had warned when I told him I would like to drive down and fish the next day. "The weather makes our winter striper fishing a risky proposition for anyone who has to travel far for it," he added. My home at Troy in the central part of the state is a good 150 miles from Virginia Beach. I had already made one fruitless trip to the beach earlier in the month. The wind had forced us to scrub our fishing then, and Claude was reluctant for me to risk another run until the weather was more promising.

But it was late December and I knew that fall and winter run of stripers could not last much longer. My oldest daughter, Pam, lives in Virginia Beach and teaches in the city school system. I decided to take a chance; three hours after hanging up the telephone, I drove into her driveway and invited myself to spend the night.

"I'll pick you up about 8 o'clock tomorrow," Claude advised when I reported my arrival. "No use in hurrying. The wind is calm now, but the water will be rough for awhile tomorrow."

I personally did not object to a little rough water, but Claude felt the fishing would be off so soon after the stormy weather.

Shortly after 8 o'clock the next morning we were speeding eastward along the Chesapeake Bay Bridge-Tunnel, headed for the Eastern Shore where Claude keeps his boat through much of the long fishing season. "Closer to the best fishing," he said, "and the launching ramp is less crowded!"

He glanced at the water. A heavy chop was still kicking up. "Wind still out of the northwest and bucking an incoming tide, but the tide will change about noon and the water will calm down. We might as well wait until then to go out. In the meantime, I'll show you some of the Eastern Shore."

In sharp contrast to the humming metropolis on the southern side of the bay where the bustling cities of Norfolk and Virginia Beach are adjacent to each other, the Eastern Shore is a charming rural community of farms and small waterfront towns. Once we left the long bridge-tunnel complex, we swung off of U.S. 13 and were suddenly in a different world. Claude followed a narrow, winding road to the little town of Oyster where we visited briefly with an ardent collector of old decoys and other artifacts of the colorful history of waterfowling along the Atlantic Coast. I could have spent hours just browsing among the hundreds of decoys, paintings, market guns, old shotgun shells, and other relics of a bygone age.

The collector was a busy waterman himself, however, so we moved on.

Our next stop was a commercial fishing and seafood company. Claude introduced me to the owner and we bought some of his freshly harvested clams. "You can take some seafood home even if we don't get any stripers," he said.

We swung back to the highway and a crowded restaurant. "The most popular eating place on the Shore," Claude said as I followed him inside. While we ate, I pumped him with questions on striped bass, and tried to learn what he thought our chances were. "The weather is against us," he said. "It is hard to hit this fishing on the head when you have only a day." Claude had tried to persuade me to come down for two or three days of fishing. "Then you are almost sure to hit at least one good day."

Lunch over, we headed for a motel where Claude kept his boat and trailer. We soon had it in tow and were en route to Kiptopeke where the Navy maintains a launching ramp for its personnel. The ramp also gets heavy use by sport and commercial fishermen. It faces the Atlantic Ocean, but is well protected by the barrier islands that extend the entire length of the long two-county peninsula that is Virginia's share of the famous Eastern Shore.

(Top) We launch Claude's big outboard. (Bottom) As we wind out of the small creek the long Chesapeake Bay Bridge-Tunnel looms in the distance.

Claude jockeyed the trailered boat into the shallow water and within minutes we were afloat and loading fishing tackle, boots and foul-weather gear aboard the big 18-foot seagoing outboard.

In spite of troublesome winds that swept cold air out of the north-west and down the broad Chesapeake Bay, it was a beautiful, crisp, sun-filled day. It was still cold, a typical late December day in Virginia, but we were dressed warmly and comfortably. In fact, the sun was so bright that Claude was concerned about sun and wind burn. He applied protective lotion to his face and offered me some.

At the turn of the starter switch, the big outboard motor purred smoothly. I was beginning to feel optimistic.

We wound slowly out of a narrow marshland creek and into a broad expanse of relatively calm water between Smith Island and the northern end of the bridge-tunnel. Once clear of the shallow water, Claude shoved the throttle forward and we sped toward the long bridge. The unprotected water of the bay was choppy, but there were no whitecaps. The big bay appeared in fair shape for fishing from the big outboard.

We passed beneath the bridge and turned left, running a course parallel to the western side of the wide span. We then slowed to cruising speed and Claude turned on his ship-to-shore radio.

I listened anxiously to the idle radio chatter, but Claude shook his head. "They are not doing anything," he mumbled. We then swung back to the ocean side of the bridge and Rogers uncased his binoculars and started glassing the water. A handful of fishing boats danced on the gently rolling bay, but none appeared to be having any luck. Occasionally we met a boat trolling slowly along the bridge pilings.

I was disappointed.

The Chesapeake Bay system has long been recognized as a prime breeding ground for the Atlantic striper fishery. Many marine biologists say it is the single most important breeding area for the anadromous fish that range the coastal waters from Nova Scotia to Florida. Known locally as rock, the striper has been popular among Chesapeake Bay anglers for years. A large resident population is boosted by the migratory fish that move in and out of the bay as they make their semiannual jaunts up and down the Atlantic Coast.

Then in the early 1960's striped bass fishing took on a refreshing new look when a rich new fishery was discovered right in the broad mouth of big Chesapeake Bay. Man and one of his engineering miracles were accidentally responsible. In 1962, the first pilings and rocky foundations were placed underwater as the "ground floor" for the long-planned Chesapeake Bay Bridge-Tunnel, built to replace the ferry system that for years had shuttled automobiles and passengers between the Virginia mainland and the Eastern Shore. The engineering package was a 17-mile combination high bridge and tunnel system with countless concrete pilings, two mile-long underwater tunnels, and four huge artificial islands. The tunnel to the north (and nearest Cape Charles on the Eastern Shore) is known as Baltimore Channel and the southern one as the Thimble Shoal Channel. The islands are numbered one to four, running south to north. Islands 1 and 2 are also known as South and North Island.

The system was opened to traffic in 1964, and in 1965 the exciting new striper fishery hit its peak along the long bridge-tunnel complex. Stripers, or rocks, true to their favorite Virginia name, fell in love with the big jumble of rocks, concrete and giant boulders. The striper fishing has continued good to this day.

(Top) Claude glasses the bay for signs of feeding fish. (Bottom) A striper boat trolls along the Chesapeake Bay Bridge-Tunnel.

Locating a school of bass is half the game in Chesapeake Bay striper fishing. The winter fish are selective feeders, but once he locates a school a good angler can usually catch fish.

Many schools are found by trolling along the bay-bridge tunnel. Hopeful anglers work both sides of the bridge and back and forth in the general vicinity of the bridge-tunnel complex.

Probably a quicker way to find stripers is to watch for feeding birds —screaming, diving and wheeling gulls. Under the birds there is usually a school of bass feasting on shiners or menhaden. The birds dive for the tidbits the feeding fish leave. That is the reason Claude brought his glasses along. He used them constantly, searching the water for signs of birds. Once a flock is located, anglers move in cautiously and cast to the school.

Skilled striper anglers also watch for oil slicks caused by feeding striped bass.

The success of fellow anglers leads many fishermen to the stripers. While no considerate angler is going to move in on a successful boat, there is nothing unethical about moving into the general area, but keeping a respectful distance. And, of course, there is always the radio network which broadcasts the actions of other boats. Many anglers locate the fish in this manner.

As we neared the middle of the bay, the bridge disappeared into the choppy blue water, but then reappeared toward the other side of the bay. "That is the North Channel Tunnel," Claude said, explaining the tunnel part of the bridge-tunnel structure. Across the wide expanse of open water a half dozen boats were anchored near the rocky artificial island.

"They are catching fish!" I exclaimed as an angler's rod bent sharply and then started vibrating.

"Tautog," said Claude.

We moved in to inquire about their luck. One happy angler reached into his fish box and held up a pair of nice fish. I snapped a couple of pictures and admired the fish. We estimated their weight at 5 or 6 pounds.

"They fish the bottom with clams," Claude replied in answer to my question concerning their fishing methods.

At that moment I would have been willing to postpone chasing stripers for a while to take part in the tautog fishing. As if to mirror my thoughts, the angler who had shown us his fish, leaned back on his rod and was battling another fish. We watched him land that one and shoved off.

As we cruised away from the tautog fishermen, Claude slowed the boat and picked up his binoculars. He focused them on a handful of boats off to our left and in the general direction of Virginia Beach.

"Rock fishermen," he said, casing his binoculars and gunning the motor for a quick run to the general vicinity of the fleet of fishing boats.

As we approached the fleet, Claude unracked a rod and handed it to me. "You fish first and let me handle the boat," I countered. "If you get a strike, I'll join you."

He made a few long, but unsuccessful casts while I maneuvered the boat.

"Birds over there!" Claude pointed back in the direction of the bridge-tunnel. I swung the boat around, but hadn't gone a hundred yards before several other boats roared in ahead of us.

"Might as well go somewhere else," muttered Claude in disgust. "They will run right into the school and make it 'sound.' That is one of our problems today with so many inexperienced fishermen on the bay."

Fishing the schools marked by the feeding gulls is much like fishing the "jumps" for white bass, a close relative of the striper. Experienced anglers watch for the birds over the stripers as white bass anglers watch for schools of small fish jumping to escape the jaws of feeding white bass. The angler must get close enough to cast to the school, but he must also maintain a safe distance so as not to frighten the fish.

I gave the wheel back to Claude and put away the rod he had rigged for me to use.

"Let's try somewhere else and get away from this crowd."

Most striped bass are migratory fish that move up and down the Atlantic Coast with the seasons. Many enter Chesapeake Bay to spawn or spend the winter, joining a large resident population that apparently moves up and down the bay and in and out of major tidal streams, but never out of the bay.

The fall stripers, leaving their homes off the coast of New England and Long Island, arrive off the coast of Virginia in early November under normal weather conditions. A few days later they begin to appear in the waters off of Virginia Beach. This signals the start of the fall and winter run of stripers in Chesapeake Bay. It is one of the most interesting seasons of the year to fish for the popular stripers.

The fall run of stripers continues through December and into the early days of January if the weather remains mild.

There is considerable doubt as to whether the migrating stripers provide all of the fall and winter action along the Chesapeake Bay Bridge-Tunnel. Many bass live out their lives in the bay. A 58-pounder taken off of Gwynn's Island near the mouth of the Rappahannock River in November several years ago set a new state record. This big fish was thought to have been a native of Chesapeake Bay rather than an immigrant from New England.

This time Claude ran the fast outboard up the bay again and under the bridge near South Island. As we broke into the open water west of the bridge, Claude muttered something under his breath. He pointed to circling gulls. "Fish under those birds," he said. This time there were only a few boats working the school.

"Likely small fish," said Claude as he handed me a rod and told me to bump the lure along the bottom. The feeding gulls drifted nearer and I started fishing eagerly.

(Top) Part of our catch of school stripers. (Bottom) Tautog fishermen hit it rich near bridge-tunnel complex.

My first cast produced nothing. Again I cast to the water behind our drifting boat, and started the jerk-and-pause retrieve that was supposed to do the trick.

Suddenly my rod doubled and I struck back! "Got a fish!" I yelled to Claude.

Striped bass are not noted for their aerial maneuvers, but they are tough fighters and very scrappy. Surface rolls, boils and threshing feature their combat tactics.

"Got a net?" I called to Claude as I worked the fish to the boat.

"Don't think you will need one. The fish is not that big." I refused to be disappointed, and swung a good 2-pounder aboard.

Those fish were not large, but it was fast, exciting fishing and I felt we could have filled the fish box had we desired. In opening paragraphs of this chapter I described our departure for bigger fish.

As we took off in search of the proverbial pot of gold, I started a discussion regarding the proper lures for winter fishing. I had used a bucktail with good success in our encounter with the school of stripers.

It was not until the early 1950's that anglers learned to catch the big schools of stripers that winter in Chesapeake Bay. The winter fish are more selective in their feeding habits, but there are a handful of proven lures that, properly presented, can be a striper's undoing. Probably the most popular of them all is the bucktail. It is used as a trolling lure and is equally effective as a casting bait. A pork-rind strip helps, and yellow and white are the preferred colors—though I had used a red one with good success. Sizes and styles vary considerably and every angler has his pets—but they all catch stripers.

Spoons give the bucktails stiff competition. Some are dressed with feathers, and old favorites include the Cathers, Nungessers and the Tony Accettas.

Trollers also use a variety of plugs. Popular ones include the Rebel, Creek Chub and Atom plug.

Surgical tubing from the medical storerooms made the striper fishing scene a few years ago and it has proven effective and popular as a substitute for eels, a favorite striper bait. While surgical eels are on the market today, many anglers still make their own, favoring the beige color that approached the hue of the live eel. The beige colors are also available in tackle shops, along with greens, purples, reds and blacks. Other imitations include plastic eels and dressed eel skins.

Regardless of the lure used, it should be worked slowly for the winter stripers are already sluggish as winter and dormancy approach.

As we moved slowly along the western side of the bridge-tunnel in the general direction of the Eastern Shore, I could not help but feel a bit pessimistic about our chances of catching a truly big striper.

The lunker hunters spend many hours between fish, and they often return home empty-handed. However, the Chesapeake Bay Bridge-Tunnel is the most likely place in the Bay to catch a lunker striper. Fish in the 30—40-pound class are not uncommon in these productive waters.

The bridge-tunnel experts say night fishing is often more productive than the more conventional daytime angling. The daylight lunker angler fishes deep—usually just a few inches above the tubes that form the long underwater tunnels. The novice to this kind of fishing will lose a lot of lures in the rocks and bridge pilings. On the other hand, the night angler can use plugs and fish fairly close to the surface where the fish feed as the lights from the bridge lure baitfish to the surface.

I had my doubts about my own ability to fish the tunnel tubes in the proper manner with such limited experience and time to practice. While I was confident that Claude could do the trick, I was sure he felt the need for a more experienced striper fisherman as a partner.

While Claude and I were chasing those stripers, my fellow Virginia hunters were enjoying the best deer season in the history of deer hunting in the state. I hated to miss even a day of what many consider the prime weeks of the hunting season. But the "Old Dominion" hunter has to make sacrifices if he plans to take advantage of the winter striper run. That was one of the reasons I had not agreed to spend more time on the bay.

There are a few stripers around the bridge-tunnel all year and anglers take them practically year-around. However, the fall and early winter months are prime ones with March and April also good as the fish start to stir again—making spawning runs up the major tidal rivers and out of the bay for northern waters.

As we approached the high span of the bridge near the Eastern Shore, Claude revved the motor and we sped under the bridge and out toward the Atlantic. Fishing can be good in the ocean waters off the tip of the Eastern Shore and east of Fishermans Island. We slowed to cruising speed and searched the water for some kind of activity that would lead us to a school of stripers. After checking out some misleading bird activity, Claude swung the boat around and we headed for Kiptopeke just as a cold sunset was forming beyond the now distant Chesapeake Bay Bridge-Tunnel.

Darkness was descending upon the marshes as we loaded the boat on the trailer and pulled away from the launching ramp.

By the time we had dropped off the boat and headed south along the bridge, bright lights were beckoning from the Virginia Beach side of the bay. I felt a sense of contentment and satisfaction as we breezed along. We had not caught any records, but few anglers are so privileged. I had stripers for my freezer, and by the time they were consumed, autumn would come again to Chesapeake Bay and the stripers would be home from New England. Maybe I would find the time to land a record striped bass, too.

INDEX

INDEX